COLORADO
HIGH ROUTES

8/29/86

Chip —

you were wonderful

you made this week one we'll

never ever forget.

Janice Pan

UCSD

COLORADO HIGH ROUTES

Aspen-Vail-Crested Butte Ski Tours
Including the Tenth Mountain Trail

Louis W. Dawson, II

The Mountaineers
Seattle

THE MOUNTAINEERS: Organized 1906
"... to explore, preserve and enjoy
the natural beauty of the Northwest."

©1986 by Louis W. Dawson, II
All rights reserved

Published by The Mountaineers
306 Second Avenue West, Seattle, Washington 98119

Published simultaneously in Canada by
Douglas & McIntyre Ltd.
1615 Venables Street, Vancouver, B.C. V5L 2H1

Manufactured in the United States of America

Copyedited by Sharon Bryan
Designed by Marge Mueller
Maps by Debbie Newell
Cover photo: Hayden Peak (Michael Kennedy photo)
Title page photo: Touring on Richmond Hill, Route 29, with Hayden Peak in
    background (Michael Kennedy photo)

Library of Congress Cataloging in Publication Data

Dawson, Louis W., II, 1952-
   Colorado high routes.

   Bibliography: p.
   Includes index.
   1. Cross-country skiing—Colorado—Guide-books.
2. Colorado—Description and travel—1981-   —Guide-
books. I. Title.
GV854.5.C6D38   1985   796.93   85-21609
ISBN 0-89886-099-7

CONTENTS

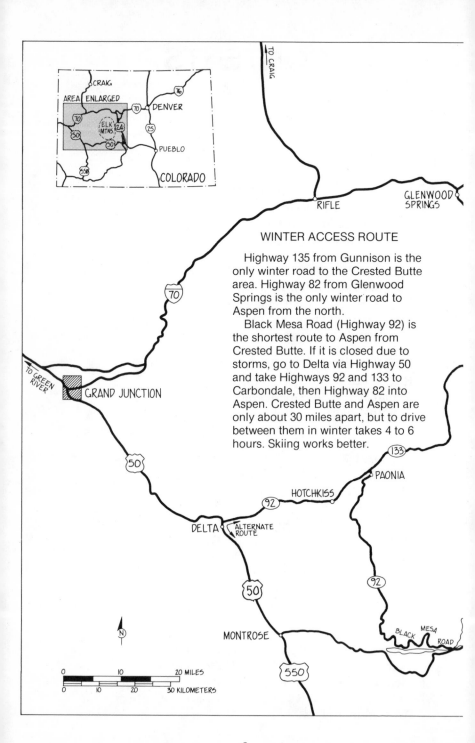

WINTER ACCESS ROUTE

Highway 135 from Gunnison is the only winter road to the Crested Butte area. Highway 82 from Glenwood Springs is the only winter road to Aspen from the north.

Black Mesa Road (Highway 92) is the shortest route to Aspen from Crested Butte. If it is closed due to storms, go to Delta via Highway 50 and take Highways 92 and 133 to Carbondale, then Highway 82 into Aspen. Crested Butte and Aspen are only about 30 miles apart, but to drive between them in winter takes 4 to 6 hours. Skiing works better.

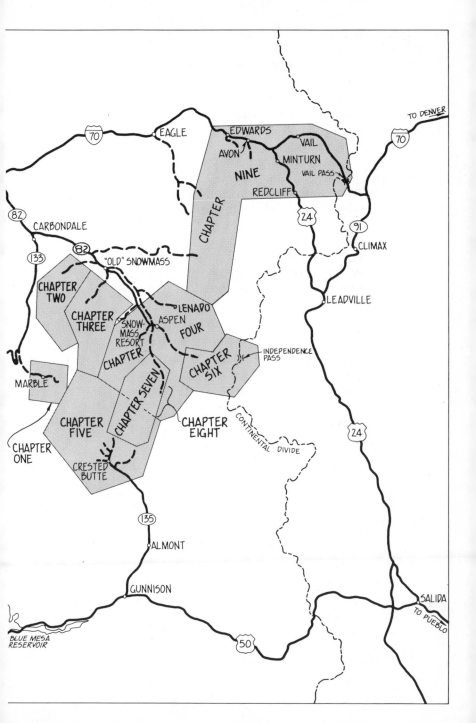

ACKNOWLEDGMENTS

This book is a labor of love by one who grew up in the Elk Mountains, and who still grows in them. Compiling the information included here required the help of many people. I would like to thank my mother, Patricia Dawson, and father, Craig Dawson; also Pauli Hayes, Peter Kelley, Michael Kennedy, Larry Pastor, Paul Ramer, Julie Peters, Lisa Spieler, Gary Sprung, Jon Waterman, and many others for their support.

Berg heil!

FOREWORD

Once a friend and I drew a circle with a 600-mile radius around Crested Butte, Colorado, and declared that there was enough mountaineering, skiing, hiking, and boating within that circle to last us a lifetime. Lou Dawson has pulled the circle quite a bit tighter, limiting it to the Elk Mountains and Sawatch Mountains, ranges in which he learned to ski and climb and which he's fond of calling "the provincial mountains."

Few people know the province better than Lou does, or are more qualified to write a guidebook to its varied ski routes. On three-pin, alpine-touring, and downhill gear, he has logged more miles in the valleys, ridges, and gullies between Aspen and Crested Butte, Taylor Park and Mount Sopris than anyone else I know. And while others have gone off to the Himalaya, Alaska, or the Blanca, Lou has paid no small amount of dues connecting high routes and ski descents in the provincial mountains. Some have been amused at his devotion to a small local range and have wondered why he hasn't followed their footsteps to distant places. The answer should be evident in this guide: it is not only a clear, concise description of tours of all degrees of difficulty, but also a testimonial to the beauty and excitement of an area that, in the winter, offers the tourer many of the problems and challenges usually associated with higher, more exotic, and costly-to-reach mountains.

Ted Kerasote,
Camping Editor, *Sports Afield*
Crested Butte

*Dedicated to my mother,
Patricia Pillsbury Dawson*

On the Elk Mountains Ridge, Route 6. (Richard Compton photo)

INTRODUCTION

Ten years ago only a score of serious ski mountaineers were enjoying the Elk Mountains and the Sawatch Mountains, and only a few casual day-tourers used the trails in the valleys of these ranges. Now a dramatic increase in the popularity of ski mountaineering is evident everywhere. This guide follows in the wake of this expanded interest. These route descriptions will help skiers get off the beaten tracks and enjoy the multitude of alternatives that the Elk and Sawatch ranges have to offer the ski mountaineer.

This book is for those who know the bite of a winter gale at the summit of a hard-earned peak, but for whom a memory is not enough, and who will always be back for more. And it is for those who have looked to the heights, but held back for lack of information on how and where to travel.

For the purpose of this guidebook the Elk Mountains are assumed to extend from Mount Sopris on the west to the Independence Pass area on the east, bordered on the north by the Roaring Fork Valley and the Williams Mountains, and on the south by the Ohio Creek drainage. The Sawatch Mountains extend between Aspen and Vail, as well as covering a large area that this guide does not include. These are generalized definitions, but will suffice here for detailing the best ski mountaineering routes in these areas.

Both ranges consist primarily of sedimentary rock and metamorphosed sedimentary rock, the most striking instance of which is known as the Maroon Formation for its distinctive coloration. The Precambrian cores of massive uplifts form the granitic peaks of the ranges. In certain areas the sedimentary rock contains fossils of small, hard-shelled marine animals. Most of the sedimentary rock at higher elevations contains few fossils of early life, but observant mountaineers may find many interesting specimens of fossilized raindrop patterns, mud cracks, and sand ripples. The igneous rock contains a wide variety of minerals. See the bibliography for books with more detailed information on these topics.

As with all other mountains in Colorado, glaciation completed the major formative processes by carving the distinctive cirques, arêtes, and steep-sided, flat-bottomed valleys characteristic of a glaciated mountain range. Presently water erosion is the only important factor in shaping the land. There are several good-sized remnants of glaciers in the Elks and Sawatch, including one in Montezuma Basin (see Route 33) and another in the Snowmass Mountain Bowl (see Route 16). These miniature glaciers show evidence of the cyclic nature of the ice ages: they wait to be fed and to grow.

Traveling Safely in the Winter Wilderness

The portion of the year when the Elk and Sawatch mountains are skiable can be divided into three "subseasons:" early winter, mid-to-late winter, and spring.

Early winter: During this period the Elks and Sawatch are characterized by thin snowpack, reduced solar radiation, and cold temperatures. It is common for an unstable layer of temperature-gradient crystals (depth-hoar) to form in the snowpack, creating difficult skiing and hazardous avalanche conditions. For the expert ski mountaineer, this is a bittersweet time: dangerous, yet subtly beautiful, with short days and long dusks and dawns. During this season, less experienced skiers would stick to the safer valley tours.

Mid-to-late winter: In this period, usually somewhere between January and early March, warmer temperatures and heavy snowfalls retard the temperature-gradient metamorphism that makes the early winter season so dangerous. The weight of the heavy snowfalls compresses the snowpack, either gluing the snow together by a process called "sintering," or triggering avalanches that slide on the temperature gradient crystal layer (TG layer). Either process can lead toward stabilization, though the former is more likely to than the latter. The problem with the latter is "repeater" avalanches on the slopes that have slid. In this circumstance, a layer of TG crystals left on the avalanche path gets covered by new or wind-transported snow, and the instability repeats. Repeater avalanches are also possible when the thin snow on the path causes a rapid reformation of the dangerous TG layer. There are times during the midwinter season when most ski trips can be safely undertaken, but these times must be pinpointed by someone skilled in avalanche hazard evaluation. A conversation with a knowledgeable ski patrolman can help skiers decide if the Elks and Sawatch are in this more stable period.

An untouched winter wilderness. (Michael Kennedy photo)

Keep in mind that this is a simplified version of the Elk Mountain "snow climate." There are many other factors that contribute to the stability of the snowpack during these different seasons, including sun crust, surface hoarfrost, and wind loading. Because there are so many different factors, it is impossible to be one hundred percent sure about any slope, so mountaineers must always remain wary. The best defense is total defense, which means avoiding avalanche slopes whenever possible and turning back at the slightest provocation (see Winter Routes).

Spring: In late March or April the snowpack warms up to temperatures around freezing, then begins to thaw. While the snow is thawing, the integrity of the snowpack is reduced and avalanches result. Fortunately, this process is cyclic and relatively predictable; the snow usually freezes at night, warms up early in the day, then does some thawing in the afternoon. While most of the snow is solidly frozen, it won't avalanche. It is important to remember that the snow may remain unfrozen after a relatively warm night, and then avalanche in the morning. This can catch the unwary because only the surface may freeze. Test this by digging or probing. More than a thin eggshell of frozen snow is necessary for stability. Staying aware of the previous night's weather and constantly checking the snow conditions during a trip will help you avoid spring avalanches.

Eventually the freezing and thawing process described above leads to a dense, consolidated snowpack that is relatively free of avalanches. This is the "mature" snow found only in the very late spring and summer at high elevations. It is distinguished by high density and uniformity. On extremely warm days there can be stability problems with this type of snow, but it is usually predictably safe.

Spring is the time to ski all routes in the Elks described as extremely difficult, and it is certainly the most enjoyable time to ski the summits. Most experienced skiers agree that while the winter offers unique and beautiful experiences, a run down a mountain on perfect spring corn snow is the ultimate ski mountaineering experience.

These subseasons vary greatly from year to year, and pinpointing them is complicated by many factors. But it is important to know what type of snowpack you are dealing with. For this type of evaluation, keep your own records of crucial factors, including snowfall, wind activity, and avalanche cycles. Supplement your own mountaineering experience with these records, and gain

A small and dangerous hard slab pocket avalanche near Pearl Pass, Route 32. (Lou Dawson photo)

additional knowledge by reading and taking courses in avalanche   )
safety. An occasional conversation with a knowledgeable ski
patrolman can be helpful. The Forest Service also provides a daily
avalanche warning that will give skiers a sense of prevailing
conditions (see Appendix C).

Hazards

Avalanche: The snow avalanche is the hazard wilderness
skiers are most likely to encounter. Avalanches are relatively
unpredictable (especially for the layman). There are numerous
examples in the literature of well-prepared and educated experts in
the field who were dead wrong. Careful route finding should be
used to avoid avalanche terrain whenever possible. Unfortunately, most routes in a mountainous area such as the Elks or
Sawatch pass below or cross over avalanche paths (even most of
the main roads are crossed by an occasional slide path). So it is
necessary for the ski mountaineer to practice "avalanche hazard
evaluation." The keynote for hazard evaluation is education, and
novices can begin by studying the excellent avalanche books in

Top left: *Examining an avalanche fracture line. Why did it slide? (Michael Kennedy photo)*. Top right: *Studying the snow to estimate avalanche danger is a task anyone can do with proper training. The results are inexact, but useful for good judgment. (Michael Kennedy photo)*. Bottom: *An avalanche path on Hayden Peak. (Lou Dawson photo)*

the bibliography. They should combine this study with experience, advice from others, and a healthy dose of caution. They should then be able to pinpoint periods of lower risk, when it is safest to travel.

All the route descriptions in this guide include information in boldface type about avalanche hazard. For purposes of this general evaluation, it is assumed that each route is being traveled during a period of moderate avalanche danger. Naturally, *this information should be used only as a guideline, and should be modified by your own ongoing hazard evaluations.*

The text often recommends that skiers "take normal precautions." This means having avalanche transceivers and knowing how to use them, carrying a good shovel, traveling one at a time in any suspect area—including runout zones—and, in short, being extremely cautious with this unpredictable hazard.

It should be noted that, though avalanches are a major hazard, many accidents in the backcountry are the result of skiing out of control and without regard for hidden obstacles. To ski safely in the wilderness it is necessary to practice "survival skiing." To survival-ski means to ski in control—anticipating hazards, falling as little as possible, and if a fall is inevitable, doing it in such a way that the consequences are not serious. Practice survival skiing at the ski resort, then take it with you into the back country.

Loose rock: Another hazard common to the Elks and Sawatch is the extremely loose rock. This problem can be encountered while climbing a peak and occasionally while crossing a pass. Take the precaution of not climbing above other skiers, and stay off steeper rock. If you do find yourself on dangerous rock, backtrack and look for a safer line. The rotten rock of the Maroon Formation is no place for bravado.

Weather: Winter in the Elks and Sawatch, as in all the Rocky Mountains, is a harsh, unforgiving time. Temperatures can drop below -40°F, yet some days in winter will roast the overdressed mountaineer as if it were mid-July. The high-altitude areas of the range are exposed to extreme winds, and moist air from the Pacific Ocean drops great quantities of snow over the central areas. Occasional thaws can have disastrous effects on the snowpack, producing avalanches and difficult skiing. The winter climate is generally cyclic; if conditions are bad, good weather will appear in a short time—almost always within three to five days.

In a discussion of mountain hazards it must be emphasized that no amount of written material can substitute for hard experience.

It can only be complementary. If you are learning ski mountaineering, gradually increase the difficulty of your excursions, methodically integrating knowledge from the printed word with that gained from experience.

Winter Routes

The factors that will influence your choice of good winter routes in the Elks and Sawatch include the density of timber and deadfall, the difficulties of breaking trail in deep snow, avalanche hazard, the frequency of stream crossings, and your own orienteering skills.

Dense forests and deadfall timber can ruin a trip, but most of the valleys in the ranges have excellent summer trails cut through the forest. To find these trails, use your map carefully and watch for trail signs such as blazes chopped into trees and sawed-off branches. Take the extra effort to stay on the trail; it is worth it in the long run.

Breaking trail is mostly hard work, but there are a few things that can help with the labor. Because breaking deep trail is like constantly climbing a hill, using climbing skins or waxing a bit warmer for traction will save you a great deal of energy. Be extra careful to set a rhythmic pace and change the lead often. Remember to eat regularly, as breaking deep trail is one of the most energy-consuming activities in ski mountaineering.

Since the Elks and Sawatch are exposed to a great deal of wind, it is often possible (especially above timberline) to find a route blown clear of snow, thereby eliminating both trail breaking and avalanche hazard. These routes are most often found on the windward sides of the high ridges. In addition to wind-scoured areas, places where the wind has compacted the snow into a surface that is safe and easily skied can be found in the high bowls and occasionally below timberline. Skiers should be aware of possible hard-slab avalanche danger in these conditions. For more information, consult the excellent avalanche books in the bibliography.

Because of frequent warm spells, open streams can be encountered in the Elks and Sawatch any time during the winter. If you are following a summer trail, there may be a log crossing or footbridge, so take the time to look. If there is no permanent bridge, look for a snow bridge or solid ice. But be careful, since these are often more form than substance. If all else fails, wade or rock-hop across. Rock-hopping is not a great alternative, since the rocks in a winter stream often have a slick coating of ice—you might end up wading unintentionally. Wading is pure torture, but safe if done carefully. The best way to wade is by wearing your boots with no socks or inner boot. If your boots are leather they may absorb a little moisture, but chances are they will not end up much wetter than they were before you started. If you have plastic boots the water will be no problem at all—just pour it out once you're across. After wading, take care to warm each other's feet, and be sure that circulation is good before continuing on the trail.

Orienteering

Map reading in the Elks and Sawatch is straightforward, since there are prominent landmarks, but ski mountaineers new to these areas will find that following most of the routes requires a fair degree of skill. To become a good map reader, use this book to plan a careful escalation in the difficulty of your route-finding excursions. Remember that no one becomes a seasoned trailblazer in one winter—it takes years, perhaps a lifetime. Have the humility not to let dogged determination prevent the constant reassessment that a skilled mountaineer should apply to every situation. Be willing to turn back!

Equipment

Ski mountaineering equipment—especially ski gear—has evolved rapidly in the past decade. Mountaineers ski on everything from nordic racing skis to "full-on" alpine gear with nonlift bindings. Traditional nordic-style touring usually involves the use of X-C ski wax. Though useful on the more gradual grade of the Tenth Mountain Trail and snow-covered roads in the Elks and Sawatch, wax rarely provides enough traction for climbing steeper grades with a pack. Climbing skins solve this problem and should be part of the skiers equipment for most of the routes described here.

To utilize this book and enjoy the routes the mountaineer should be aware of his skill level with the equipment he chooses to use, and apply this awareness to the difficulty grades described on page 24.

The clothing, ski gear and camping gear in general use these days is superb. Yet remember that gear can break. Analyze the weaknesses in your equipment and carry a well-thought-out emer-

Left: *Blue diamonds are used to mark some cross-country ski trails. As with all man-made markings, they lack reliability.* Right: *Trails are sometimes marked with notches on trees called blazes. These marks are usually easy to spot, but sometimes natural scarring can be mistaken for a blaze. (Lou Dawson photos)*

gency repair kit that includes essential spare parts and tools for your ski bindings, fire starting equipment, and clothing repair.

Emergency Procedures

Every party venturing into the winter wilderness should be sure that each participant has some degree of skill in first and secondary aid. This is best accomplished by taking an advanced first-aid course and studying books such as *Medicine for Mountaineering* (see bibliography). As well as first-aid knowledge, backcountry skiers should be well versed in the various methods of moving an injured person on snow. Accidents often happen in places where members of the group have to move the victim to a safe bivouac site or helicopter landing area. The author recommends practicing these evacuation techniques; they generally work better on paper than on snow.

A well-planned and expedient rescue-evacuation begins with the victim and the companions in the field. If this initial phase is executed properly, the mountain rescue team can follow through with great efficiency. Most immobilizing medical problems in the winter wilderness require a helicopter for an evacuation, though a rescue group will occasionally use a snowmobile or ski patrol-type sled. Whatever method is finally used, the sequence of action should follow these guidelines:

1. Someone in civilization should know of your route plan and schedule, so they can notify authorities if you are overdue. Even so, if something goes wrong you can't count on rescuers appearing, so you will need to take other steps.
2. Do the proper first aid to stabilize the ill or injured person's condition, and if necessary move him.
3. If you decide you need a rescue, you will have to send someone out to notify authorities. If there are only two of you, be sure the injured person is warm, comfortable, and safe, before the other leaves.
4. Be sure the person who goes out has a USGS map well marked with the location of the victim and a description of the accident and injuries written in the margin.
5. The person who goes out should ski conservatively and reserve sufficient energy to be able to communicate with the rescue group and possibly to fly back in with them to help locate the victim.
6. To notify authorities, simply call the sheriff in whatever county the victim is located (see Appendix C). The sheriff will take it from there.
7. If you do need a rescue, a helicopter may fly in. For a landing site, select and mark an open area as near as possible to your bivouac. The site can be marked by a large circle stamped in the snow and brightly colored gear strewn about. A smoky fire can help by acting as a signal and showing wind direction, but do not depend on this alone, and do not build it in the middle of the landing site!

Remember that the more life-threatening the situation, the more important a calm and collected attitude is to a successful resolution.

How to Use This Guide

The ski routes are described and numbered consecutively. Cross referencing is by number. All the loop trips are described as if they were skied from the direction that provides the most efficient travel with regard to navigation, road heads, and physical effort. Each route description includes the following information: maps, estimated travel time and distance, starting elevation, and elevation gain. Each trip is rated according to difficulty of the climb and the mountaineering skill level necessary to do the route safely: novice, intermediate, advanced, and extreme. These ratings are for winter conditions, unless the route is recommended only for the spring.

A novice route is safe for ski mountaineers who are just past being beginners, and who can decipher a map if they take the time. The route will not require a night out and does not have difficult downhill skiing.

Skiers who take on an intermediate route should have some experience with winter camping and survival, and be familiar with intermediate-level downhill skiing. Some map-reading skill is necessary. Skiers on an intermediate route should have a fair degree of mountaineering judgment.

Skiers on an advanced route should have a high degree of skill with all aspects of ski mountaineering other than extreme skiing. "Extreme skiing" refers to ski descents where an uncontrolled fall would lead to certain injury or death.

Skiers on an extreme route should be skilled in extreme skiing and technical climbing. The extreme route is definitely the outer fringe of the sport, though it can be done safely in the right conditions, and with the necessary knowledge and equipment.

This is not a "how-to" book for back-country skiing but a guidebook for the confirmed ski mountaineering enthusiast. It does not include descriptions of the snow-covered roads, trails, and golf courses that are the stepping stones of the neophyte and the stomping ground of the nordic ski racer. The book can be used by beginners, though, since sections of many of the trips make excellent easy day tours. To help you find them, Appendix A lists the routes that begin with good novice terrain. Local guide services and ski shops can direct beginners to practice tracks. For instruction in ski mountaineering, good guides and classes are available in Aspen, Vail, and Crested Butte (see Appendix C). Information on maintained nordic ski trails is available from local guide services.

The route descriptions and maps here are intended to be used in combination with full-size USGS 7.5 minute, 1:2400 topographical maps. Number-letter combinations in parentheses in the text correspond to those found on the maps in this book. The routes are also marked with a dark line and their reference number from the text. For road routes, use the topo maps and the maps in this book along with Forest Service maps for the Gunnison and White River national forests. All these maps are available at local mountaineering stores and Forest Service regional offices, or by mail from the United States Geological Survey (see Appendix C).

Chapter 9, which describes the Tenth Mountain Trail between Aspen and Vail Pass, is written to be self-contained and easily separated from the remainder of the guidebook. Therefore, cross-references to other chapters have been avoided in favor of a degree of redundancy in the descriptions.

The descriptions are based primarily on personal knowledge. Combined with a map, they set forth quite a bit of useful information, but they are not an inch-by-inch accounting of the trails. You will find a sufficient amount of detail to allow the enjoyment of the routes in the traditional mountaineering sense— that is, a feeling of adventure combined with enough safety to ensure your being able to enjoy the mountains another day. *Colorado High Routes* is intended primarily as a supplement to good judgment.

Selected avalanche slopes are marked on the maps, however it would be impossible to mark all avalanche slopes.

Ski touring near Conundrum Creek, Aspen. (Richard Compton photo)

CHAPTER ONE

Routes from Marble

There is a great deal of excellent alpine touring terrain around the small town of Marble. Unfortunately, with the exception of lower Yule Creek (Route 1), the area has far too many avalanche paths to be safe in the winter. The spring season is the recommended time for skiing the peaks in this area.

To get to Marble, drive Colorado Highway 82 from either Glenwood Springs or Aspen and turn off on Highway 133, the road to Carbondale, Redstone, and McClure Pass. Drive past Carbondale and up the long valley for about 21 miles. On your left, about a mile before the long switchback up McClure Pass, you will see a prominent sign marking the turn onto the Marble Road. Drive this road six miles to the small town of Marble, so named because of the fine marble that was once quarried a ways up Yule Creek.

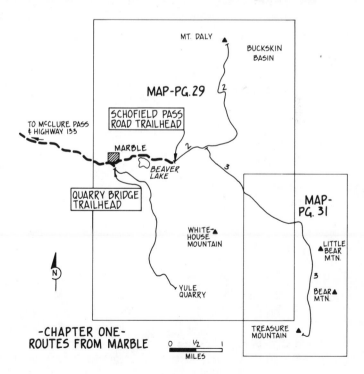

1   Yule Creek from Marble

Difficulty: Novice
Time: 6 hours round trip
Distance: 6 ½ miles round trip
Elevation gain: 1,000 feet
Starting elevation: 7,956 feet
USGS 7.5 minute map: Marble

Map—page 29

From the middle of the town of Marble, follow Third Street to the south. You will soon come to a snowplow turnaround and a small bridge, the Quarry Bridge. A sign at the plow turnaround says National Historic Site. Cross the Quarry Bridge and ski the road that climbs up this side of the valley. In about ¾ of a mile, the road will turn right into the Yule Creek drainage. Follow this road up the valley for about three miles, and you will soon arrive at the fascinating marble quarries. Give yourself some time to explore the area, then return via the same route. It is possible to continue up Yule Creek past the quarries. This portion is not recommended because it crosses many avalanche paths that run out into the valley and the route finding is very difficult.

Avalanche notes: This is a very safe trip.

2   Mount Daly from Marble

Difficulty: Intermediate
Time: 8 hours round trip
Distance: 6 miles round trip
Elevation gain: 3,600 feet
Starting elevation: 8,000 feet
USGS 7.5 minute map: Marble

Map—page 29

To avoid confusion, it should be noted that there are two Mount Dalys in the Elks, this one and the one next to Capitol Peak (Routes 9 and 10). This one near Marble is one of the finest ski mountains in the Elks. To climb Daly, drive through Marble and past Beaver Lake, then head east up the main valley on the Schofield Pass Road. Early in the year the road is closed near what is marked as Daniels Hill on the USGS *Marble* map, but later in the spring you can drive beyond that. At the top of Daniels Hill

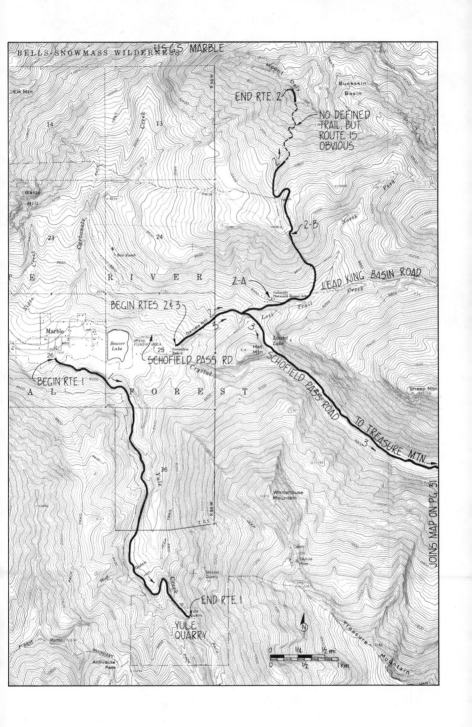

BELLS-SNOWMASS WILDERNESS   USGS MARBLE

Elk Mtn

Gallo Hill

END RTE 2

NO DEFINED TRAIL, BUT ROUTE IS OBVIOUS

Buckskin Basin

Moose

2-B

2-A

LEAD KING BASIN ROAD

Colorado Outward Bound Sch

BEGIN RTES 2 & 3

Devils Pnt

SCHOFIELD PASS RD

STATE FISHING AREA

Snowshoe Bench

Marble

Beaver Lake

BEGIN RTE 1

RIVER

Hat Mtn

Lizard Lake

SCHOFIELD PASS ROAD

TO TREASURE MTN

Sheep Mtn

AL   FOREST

Whitehouse Mountain

Yule

END RTE 1

YULE QUARRY

Anthracite Pass

BOUNDARY

N

0   ¼   ½ mi
½   1 km

Treasure Mountain

JOINS MAP ON PG. 3

It's nice to ski without a pack sometimes! (Michael Kennedy photo)

turn left on a spur off the main road and travel to the small intermittent stream about a half-mile past the Colorado Outward Bound School (2-A). Leave the spur road here and follow the stream up toward Point 10,690 on the USGS map. About a hundred vertical feet below the top of the point, begin a contour to the right (2-B). Soon you will hit the small low-angled area that is next to the word "trail" on the USGS map. From here climb directly to the summit via any one of a number of small ridges.

It is possible to ski back down the ascent route, but the best skiing is to be found by dropping east from the summit into Buckskin Basin. Follow the basin drainage down into the North Fork drainage. Then ski the North Fork Valley until the bushwhacking becomes too difficult at about the 9,400-foot level. To avoid misery here, simply ski to the southwest and intersect the intermittent stream where you began the ascent.

It is possible to ski the basin several times in one day by traversing back to the ascent route via the pack trail marked on the USGS map. One note of caution: there are a number of cliffs on the

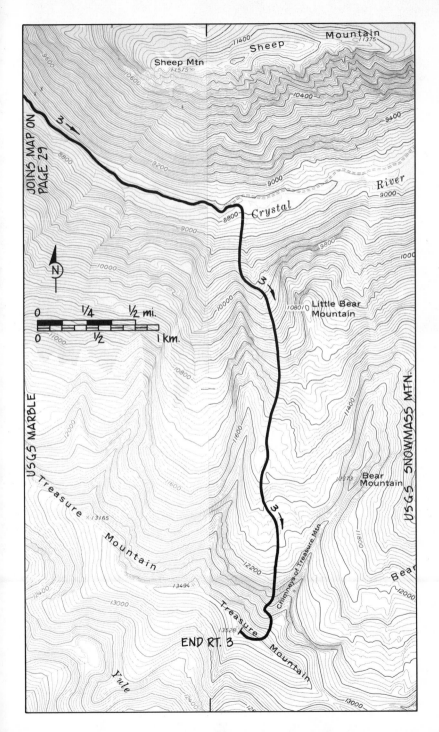

east ridge (the ridge forming the south side of Buckskin Basin). Take care to avoid these if you traverse back for another run.

Avalanche notes: Since all the good skiing on Mount Daly is in avalanche terrain, it should only be skied during the most stable times. Buckskin Basin is threatened by a south-facing mountainside that can thaw out and avalanche quite early on a spring morning. In winter, the ascent route provides the safest downhill skiing.

3 Treasure Mountain

Difficulty: Advanced
Time: 6 hours round trip
Distance: 5 miles
Elevation gain: 4,700 feet
Starting elevation: 8,800 feet
USGS 7.5 minute maps: Marble, Snowmass Mountain

Maps—pages 29 and 31

There is an excellent steep ski gully that drops off to the north from the summit of Treasure Mountain. As with most steep ski descents, it is best to climb up via the descent route. To accomplish this, simply hike or drive (depending on the snow) about four miles up the Schofield Pass Road out of Marble. Leave the road here and climb up the pronounced avalanche chute that leads into the basin formed by Bear Mountain and Treasure Mountain. Little Bear Mountain will be on your left as you climb up the first thousand vertical feet from the road. After this you will be heading up toward the unusual formations called the "Chimneys of Treasure Mountain" on the USGS *Snowmass Mountain* map. The remainder of the route follows the gully that is next to the ridge with the chimneys. This last portion is fairly steep and should be approached with caution.

Avalanche notes: This is a long climb, especially if you have to walk much of the road from Marble. It might be wise to camp at the base of the gully in order to make the requisite early morning start to avoid avalanches from thawing snow. This route is only safe in spring frozen-snow conditions.

Climbing the east ridge of Mount Sopris. The bowl on the right may be skied. (Michael Kennedy photo)

CHAPTER TWO

Mount Sopris Area

The imposing bulk of Mount Sopris, visible from the Roaring Fork Valley between Glenwood Springs and Basalt, forms the western bastion of the Elk Mountains. The mountain offers fantastic skiing. It has great vertical drops, and skiable routes lie in almost every direction from the three summits. The area surrounding the peak provides some of the best intermediate touring in the Elks.

In the winter, the mountain is known for its high winds and unstable weather, but its safe, easily navigated ridge routes make

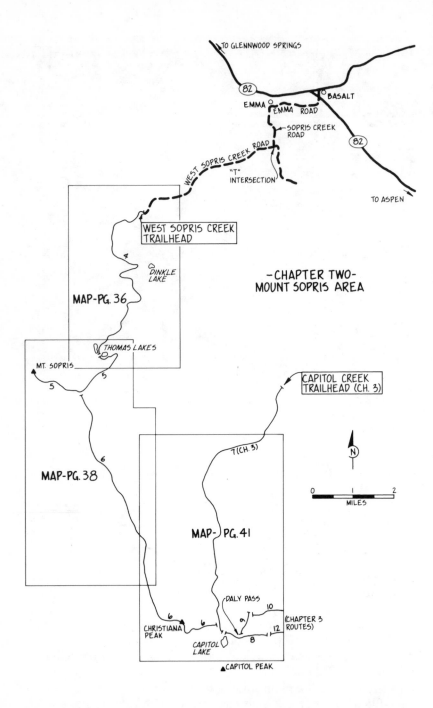

TO GLENNWOOD SPRINGS

82

EMMA   EMMA   ROAD   BASALT

SOPRIS CREEK
ROAD

WEST SOPRIS CREEK ROAD

"T"
INTERSECTION

82

TO ASPEN

WEST SOPRIS CREEK
TRAILHEAD

4

DINKLE
LAKE

-CHAPTER TWO-
MOUNT SOPRIS AREA

MAP-PG. 36

THOMAS LAKES

MT. SOPRIS

5

5

CAPITOL CREEK
TRAILHEAD (CH. 3)

7 (CH. 3)

N

0   1   2
MILES

MAP-PG. 38

6

MAP- PG. 41

DALY PASS

10

(CHAPTER 3
ROUTES)

6   6

12

CHRISTIANA
PEAK

8

CAPITOL
LAKE

CAPITOL PEAK

Sopris a rewarding and relatively easy ski-climb. Sopris is good in the winter, but it is best in the spring, when skiers can take advantage of the mountain's big drops. The spring season's corn snow, stable weather, and predictable avalanche conditions make for ideal skiing.

4 Thomas Lakes from West Sopris Creek Road

Difficulty: Intermediate
Time: 6 hours one way
Distance: 6 miles
Elevation gain: 2,500 feet
Starting elevation: 7,600 feet
USGS 7.5 minute maps: Mount Sopris, Basalt

Map—page 36

The best staging point for skiing on Mount Sopris is the Thomas Lakes area, around the three lakes to the northeast of the summit. The ski to the lakes, from the West Sopris Creek roadhead, follows a snow-covered jeep trail most of the way and is fairly easy. The only problem with the route is the occasional snowmobile.

To reach the West Sopris Creek roadhead, coming from the direction of Aspen, take Highway 82 to the small town of Basalt. Just before the town you will come to a bridge that takes Highway 82 across the Roaring Fork River. The Basalt High School will be on your right. A few feet *before* crossing this bridge, take an unmarked turn to the left. Follow this road over another bridge and about two miles to the small town of Emma. Drive through Emma, then take a hard left onto the Sopris Creek Road, where there is a small road sign. After you turn onto the Sopris Creek Road, you can see the summits of Capitol Peak and Mount Daly peeking over the ridge straight ahead. Follow the road for a mile to a "T," take a right, and you will be on the West Sopris Creek Road. As you drive, Mount Sopris will be visible directly ahead. Follow this road four miles to the snowplow turnaround. There is a white ranch house here on the left side of the road (the road from this point may be privately plowed—drive at your own risk). There is no place to park overnight at the winter roadhead, so have a friend drop you off and arrange for a pickup if necessary. In the spring there is parking at the trailhead.

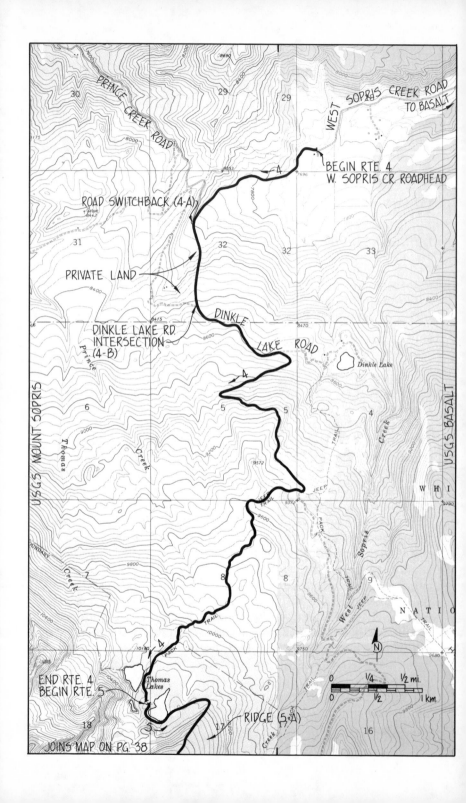

The skiing portion of the route stays on the snow-covered road for a mile, to a sharp turn where the road switchbacks to the right (north) (4-A). Leave the main road at this turn and follow a more obscure road to the south for a few hundred yards, until you come to a barbed wire fence and gate. Do not cross over the private land, simply follow the fence to the left and head up the hill to intersect the Dinkle Lake Road (4-B) as shown on the USGS *Mount Sopris* map.

Follow the Dinkle Lake Road to a point about ¼ of a mile before Dinkle Lake. Here, take the trail fork to the right that climbs toward Thomas Lakes. About 1 ½ miles up this trail, take another fork to the right and follow this to the lakes. Be sure to read your map well, as the roads and trails in this area are not well marked. Be aware that false trails may be set by wandering snowmobilers.

Avalanche notes: Be careful of exposed camping at Thomas Lakes.

5   Sopris Summits from Thomas Lakes

Difficulty: Intermediate
Time: 4 hours to the main summits
Distance: 3 miles
Elevation gain: 2,500 feet
Starting elevation: 10,200 feet
USGS 7.5 minute map: Mount Sopris

Map—page 38

At Thomas Lakes (see Route 4) the ski mountaineer is in perfect position for a climb to the three summits of Mount Sopris. On the southeast side of the lakes, a prominent wide ridge (5-A) rises to the easternmost summit of the mountain. The crest of this ridge is safe from avalanches and is skiable up to the last several hundred feet. Staying on the safe line does force you to scramble over some rocks. Once on the east summit, you can reach the main summits by walking or skiing along the summit ridge. The descent is by the same route, or one of the northeast bowls if conditions are deemed safe for skiing avalanche terrain.

Avalanche notes: This is a safe winter route if care is taken to avoid cornice overhangs.

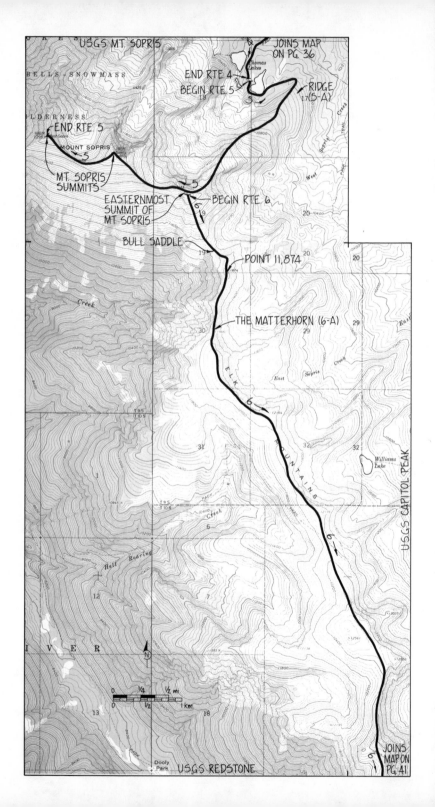

USGS MT SOPRIS

JOINS MAP ON PG. 36

BELLS - SNOWMASS

END RTE 4

BEGIN RTE 5

RIDGE 17(5-A)

LDERNESS

END RTE 5

MOUNT SOPRIS

MT. SOPRIS SUMMITS

EASTERNMOST SUMMIT OF MT SOPRIS

BEGIN RTE 6

BULL SADDLE

POINT 11,874

THE MATTERHORN (6-A)

ELK

MOUNTAINS

USGS CAPITOL PEAK

Williams Lake

Hell Roaring

Creek

Creek

N

0   ¼   ½ mi
0   ½   1 km

USGS REDSTONE

Dooly Park

JOINS MAP ON PG. 41

MT. SOPRIS

EAST SUMMIT   MAIN SUMMIT

RIDGE
(ROUTE 5)

BULL SADDLE

Mount Sopris from the north. (Gnurps photo)

6   East Sopris Summit to Capitol Lake via Elk Mountains Ridge

Difficulty: Advanced
Time: 3 days
Distance: About 10 miles
Elevation gain: 2,000 feet
Starting elevation: 12,453 feet
USGS 7.5 minute maps: Mount Sopris, Redstone, Capitol Peak

Maps—pages 38 and 41

Certainly the best high alpine ski tour in the Elks is this ridge connecting Mount Sopris with Capitol Lake. This can be an excellent trip in both winter and spring. And the additional challenge of several short scrambling sections gives the route some variety.

Begin the Elk Mountains ridge route from the east Sopris summit (see Routes 4 and 5). From there drop down south to the low point on the ridge (called Bull Saddle on the map in the text). Continue for a short distance along the ridge to a large bastion of scree and rock outcroppings (Point 11,874). Negotiate the point via a scree slope on the left, sans skis. From the summit of the point, ski the ridge crest for about ½ mile to the base of an obvious arête (6-A) that has been fondly dubbed "The Matterhorn." This little gem involves another short scramble.

Just past the Matterhorn is the broad and eminently skiable portion of the ridge. Follow this section for about seven miles to map Point 12,878, about 1 ¼ miles to the northwest of Capitol Lake. This point (not named on the USGS *Capitol Peak* map) is called Christiana Peak. Drop down the south shoulder of Christiana Peak, intersecting the first saddle to the south (6-B), the one between Christiana and the double-topped rocky bump shown on the USGS *Capitol Peak* map.

From the saddle, if avalanche conditions are favorable, drop into the bowl to the northeast (toward the Capitol Creek drainage). Ski to the 12,000-foot level in the bowl, then climb over the small ridge that forms the east side of the bowl at this level. From the crest of the small ridge (6-C), combine a bit of contouring to the east with skiing the small bowls and slopes that will lead you to a point

The view west from Bald Knob (see Route 78), showing Mount Sopris on the far right and Capitol Peak, the sharp peak to the left of center. The Elk Mountains Ridge is the high ridge connecting the two peaks. (Lou Dawson photo)

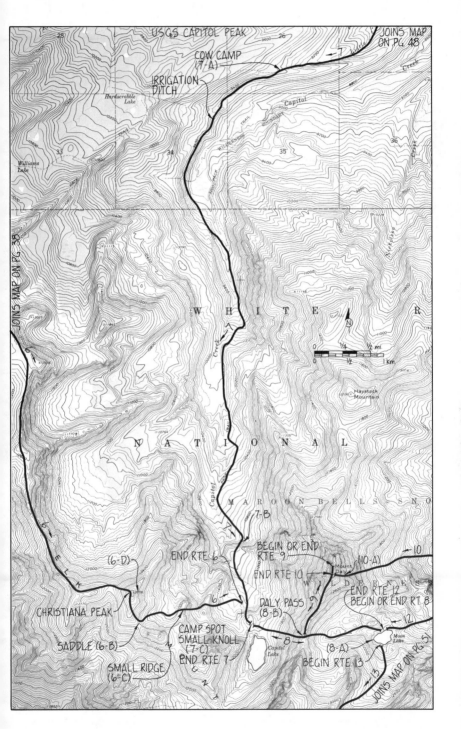

USGS CAPITOL PEAK

COW CAMP
(7-A)

IRRIGATION
DITCH

Hardscrabble Lake

Williams Lake

Capital

W   H   I   T   E   R.

Haystack Mountain

N   A   T   I   O   N   A   L

Capitol

MAROON BELLS SNO

7-B

BEGIN OR END
RTE 9

END RTE 6

(6-D)

(10-A)

10

END RTE 10

CHRISTIANA PEAK

DALY PASS
(8-B)

WILDERNESS

END RTE 12
BEGIN OR END RT. 8

SADDLE (6-B)

CAMP SPOT
SMALL KNOLL
(7-C)
END RTE 7

8

(8-A)

Moon Lake

12

SMALL RIDGE
(6-C)

Capitol Lake

BEGIN RTE 13

13

41

Elk Mountains Ridge in the foreground, with the north face of Capitol Peak looming above. (Richard Compton photo)

just below the small knoll to the north of the Capitol Lake outlet. To get back to civilization from Capitol Lake, follow Routes 8 and 12 or 7.

If snow conditions are unsafe in the open bowls and you must descend into Capitol Creek, follow a series of rocky ribs on the east face of Christiana Peak (6-D). It is possible to reach the lower part of the bowl safely if these ribs are reasonably clear of snow. Once in the low, angled portion of the bowl, descend to the point where the USGS *Capitol Peak* map shows the two intermittent streams combining. From here you can ski down a sparsely treed headwall on the south side of the creek, and continue to the point where the vegetation shading begins on the USGS map. At this point contour up valley to the east, gradually dropping into the bottom of the Capitol Creek Valley about ¾ of a mile below Capitol Lake.

Camping spots on the Elk Mountains Ridge are sparse. Bull Saddle is good, and there are occasional areas along the way that offer shelter from the wind, including a few spots for snow caves. In case of bad weather or accident, the two best routes down from the ridge are off Bull Saddle and back to the Dinkle Lake Road, or down the packtrail to the south of Williams Lake.

Avalanche notes: A thorough knowledge of avalanche hazard evaluation and safe trail selection is mandatory for this route.

Packed trails can be fun. Snowmass ski area, with Garret Peak in the background. (Michael Kennedy photo)

CHAPTER THREE

Capitol and Snowmass Lake Area

This area of the Elks, dominated by the beautiful 14,000-foot Capitol and Snowmass peaks, affords the most challenging ski mountaineering in the range. The area's valleys are extremely long and threatened by many avalanche paths, and the route finding is intricate, involving large areas of deadfall timber and steep terrain. Most winter mountaineering in this area should be undertaken only by experts, the exceptions being a few routes in the lower valley areas. Yet spring in this area is, as usual, a different matter. Groups have reported the best spring skiing in the Elks to be found on Snowmass Peak (see Route 16).

7 Capitol Creek to Capitol Lake

Difficulty: Advanced
Time: Long day or possibly overnight
Distance: 8 miles one way
Elevation gain: 3,000 feet
Starting elevation: 8,560 feet
USGS 7.5 minute maps: Basalt, Capitol Peak

Maps—pages 41 and 48

This route to Capitol Lake is very demanding in the winter, and is seldom traveled by anyone other than climbers attempting ascents of Capitol Peak. But Capitol Lake in the winter is one of the seven wonders of the Elks, making the trip well worth it for nonclimbers.

To reach the trailhead, follow Highway 82 to the Old Snowmass Road, about 16 miles west of Aspen. Turn onto this road and travel about two miles to a major "T" intersection. Take the right fork and drive to the road terminus. This will usually be near the intersection of the road spur that heads right to the building marked as the Capitol Creek Guard Station on the USGS *Capitol Peak* map. This "guard station" is actually a private ranch whose owner used to be a fire warden. Ask permission at the ranch to park your car off the road.

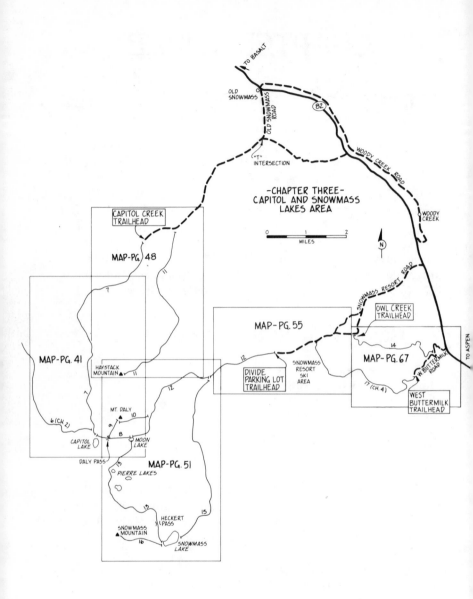

TO BASALT

OLD
SNOWMASS

OLD SNOWMASS ROAD

82

WOODY CREEK ROAD

"T"
INTERSECTION

WOODY
CREEK

—CHAPTER THREE—
CAPITOL AND SNOWMASS
LAKES AREA

0   1   2
MILES

N

CAPITOL CREEK
TRAILHEAD

MAP-PG. 48

SNOWMASS RESORT ROAD

OWL CREEK
TRAILHEAD

7

11

MAP-PG. 55

TO ASPEN

MAP-PG. 41

12

14

MAP-PG. 67

HAYSTACK
MOUNTAIN ▲ 11

DIVIDE
PARKING LOT
TRAILHEAD

SNOWMASS
RESORT
SKI
AREA

W. BUTTERMILK ROAD

7

12

17 (CH. 4)

MT. DALY
▲ 10

WEST
BUTTERMILK
TRAILHEAD

6 (CH 2)

9

8

CAPITOL
LAKE

MOON
LAKE

DALY PASS

3

MAP-PG. 51

PIERRE LAKES

13

15

SNOWMASS
MOUNTAIN ▲

HECKERT
PASS

16

SNOWMASS
LAKE

46

The ski gully on Mount Daly described in Route 10 is a little to the left of the summit. (Michael Kennedy photo)

From the intersection, continue up the road, either on skis or foot depending on the condition of the road. By staying on the road you will travel on the north side of a small ridge that separates you from the Capitol Creek drainage. After about two miles the road will climb to the left up onto the crest of this ridge at 9,440 feet (7-A). This area is called "Cow Camp" (the USGS map shows the trail forking here).

From Cow Camp you can drop directly down into the Capitol Creek drainage and ski up the trail marked on the map. To avoid losing elevation, a better route is to follow an obvious irrigation ditch that contours along the west side of the valley at 9,320 feet and leads to a sparsely timbered area about three miles up the

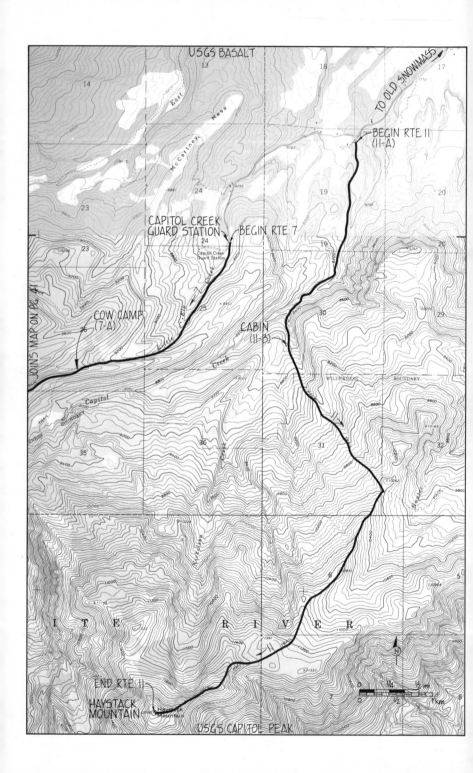

valley (just past the second swamp marked on the USGS map).

From here follow the trail marked on the USGS map, making minor deviations to avoid avalanche runouts, for about three miles to the "headwall" at 10,800 feet (7-B), an abrupt 250 vertical-feet section about a mile from the lake. The trail up the headwall, as marked on the USGS map, cuts across several small avalanche paths. To avoid these, simply ski up through the dense trees on the left (climbing skins help). At the top of the headwall, follow the trail as marked on the map for about ¼ mile, then make a major deviation by skiing directly up the drainage until you are just below the small tree-studded knoll (7-C) to the north of the lake. Ski around the right side of the knoll and pay attention to the avalanche path coming off the rocky peak up to the right. The safest and most sheltered camping is in a small depression near the top of the knoll (7-C).

Avalanche notes: There are numerous runouts crossing the route, although they are easily spotted and negotiated via their perimeters. Some big slides come off the west face of Mount Daly, which is why the winter route swings to the right here. Bear in mind that although the approach to the knoll (7-C) is threatened by some smaller slopes to the right, these are not as bad as the Daly avalanches. In the winter it is possible to travel this route in relative safety during periods of diminished avalanche activity.

8   Capitol Lake to Moon Lake via Daly Pass

Difficulty: Advanced
Time: 3 hours to Moon Lake
Distance: 2 miles
Elevation gain: 900 feet
Starting elevation: 11,600 feet
USGS 7.5 minute map: Capitol Peak

Map—page 41

Moon Lake (8-A) is the small lake (11,720 feet) at the head of West Snowmass Creek on the east side of the ridge that connects Mount Daly and Capitol Peak. The route described below is used as part of an ascent route for Mount Daly (see Route 9), and as a connector for a trip up Capitol Creek (Route 7) and down West Snowmass Creek (Route 12).

Daly Pass (8-B) is the low point on the ridge, and is obvious from both sides. As with all passes in the Elks, it is best approached from the windward side, so that you can ascend a route that is relatively safer from avalanches and descend the more dangerous slope. Since the Elks are subject to the prevailing westerlies, the windward slope will usually be the west (Capitol Lake) side.

As you study the pass from the west, you will see a slightly vegetated raised area curving up to the saddle. This is the best route, and is safest from avalanches when well wind scoured and compacted.

The east side of the pass is usually more of a problem to negotiate safely. It is often a leeward snow collection basin and usually must be approached with a degree of calculated risk. The only factors that lessen the danger are the short drop of the runout zone (less danger on the grand scale) and some rock outcroppings that can be used as islands of safety to link up a route.

The skiing from the pass down to Moon Lake can be exceptional. And there is a fair amount of good skiing from the lake to the roadhead (see Route 12). There is a great deal of interesting terrain for spring skiing on both sides of the pass.

Avalanche notes: Mountaineers with a great deal of experience finding routes in avalanche terrain can negotiate this pass fairly safely if snow distribution leaves certain areas uncovered.

9   Mount Daly Summit from Daly Pass

Difficulty: Advanced
Time: 2 ½ hours round trip from Daly Pass
Distance: 2 miles round trip
Elevation gain: 900 feet
Starting elevation: 12,480 feet
USGS 7.5 minute map: Capitol Peak

Map—page 41

This is one of the best winter climbs in the Elks for the experienced skier who is not a technical climber. The route is simple: after gaining Daly Pass by Routes 7 and 8, hike the crest of the ridge that leads from the pass to the summit. The return is by the same route. Most climbers leave their skis at the pass because the ridge is steep, rocky, and usually blown clear of snow.

Avalanche notes: The route following the crest of the ridge has virtually no avalanche danger, but beware of cornices.

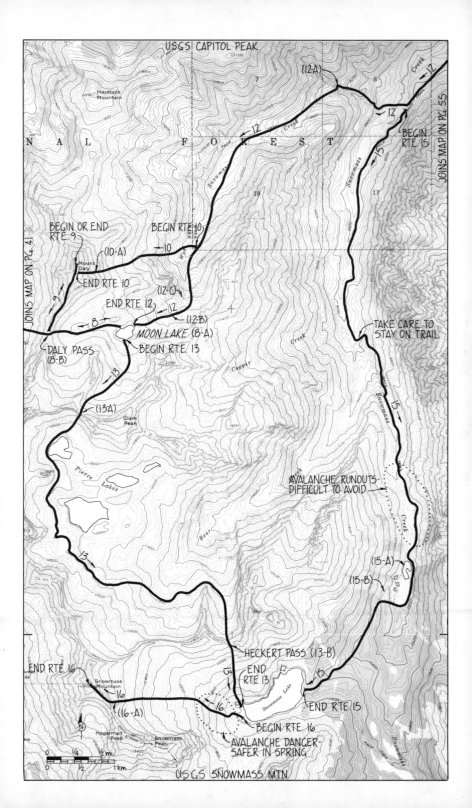

10   East Face of Mount Daly

Difficulty: Extreme
Time: 8 hours round trip from Divide parking lot
Distance: 6 miles from the Divide parking lot
Elevation gain: 4,800 feet
Starting elevation: 8,920 feet
USGS 7.5 minute map: Capitol Peak

Map—page 51

This is an excellent spring ski descent that descends a beautiful gully (10-A) on the east side of Mount Daly, beginning just south of the summit. As with other ski descents of this sort, it is best to climb the peak via the ski route for a thorough reconnaissance. This can be easily accomplished by following West Snowmass Creek (see Route 12) to the small unnamed lake below the east face of Daly (as shown on the USGS *Capitol Peak* map). From the lake, follow obvious open areas that allow you to climb up in the vicinity of the intermittent stream. You will soon reach the base of the east face, and from there the gully is easy to spot.

Avalanche notes: An early morning start after a cold spring night will ensure a minimum of danger. Consider camping close to the mountain in order to make an early start.

11   Haystack Mountain

Difficulty: Intermediate
Time: 10 hours round trip
Distance: 12 miles round trip
Elevation gain: 4,200 feet
Starting elevation: 8,000 feet
USGS 7.5 minute maps: Basalt, Capitol Peak

Map—page 48

This is a highly recommended route that includes an enjoyable summit. To find the trailhead, use the directions for the Capitol Creek Roadhead (Route 7). From the "T" intersection mentioned in the description, take a right and drive just over 4 ½ miles to an unsigned turnoff to the left (11-A). This public right-of-way is usually only plowed for a short distance. Ask for parking permission at the ranch house just past the turnoff.

The east side of Daly Pass, a short yet potentially dangerous avalanche slope. (Lou Dawson photo)

From your parking place, ski up the snow-covered road to the cabin (11-B) on the map in the text. From the cabin, follow the trail marked on the map that heads in a southeasterly direction and climbs to the obvious ridge. The trail gains the ridge at a saddle. There is often a snowmobile track to this point. From the saddle, stay on the ridge as it leads you to the summit. The only difficult navigation on the ridge is staying oriented in the flat areas, especially if the surrounding landmarks are obscured by clouds. There is good downhill skiing on either side of the lower portion of the ridge.

Avalanche notes: This route covers extremely safe terrain, but offers access to a few dangerous slopes. Stick to the ridge higher up and do your downhill skiing in the gentle meadows lower down.

12   West Snowmass Creek to Moon Lake

Difficulty: Advanced
Time: 9 hours one way
Distance: 7 miles to Moon Lake
Elevation gain: 4,000 feet
Starting elevation: 8,920 feet
USGS 7.5 minute maps: Highland Peak, Capitol Peak

Maps—pages 51 and 55

This is the most popular approach for a winter ascent of Capitol Peak, and offers another of the Elks' interesting route-finding problems. Most parties begin the trip at the Divide parking lot near the Snowmass Resort ski area. To reach this parking lot, drive down the valley from Aspen about six miles on Highway 82. Take the Snowmass Resort turnoff on the left (not to be confused with Old Snowmass farther down the valley). Follow this road up past the Snowmass Resort. The Divide Road will head to the right about ½ mile past the turnoff to the resort. All these junctions are well signed. There is no free or overnight parking here, so have a friend drop you off.

From the parking lot, ski down the cat track that leads to the west, and stay on the track as it leads you to a boundary rope on the up-valley side of the ski slopes near the valley floor. Do not be overly concerned if you miss this; in that case ski up through

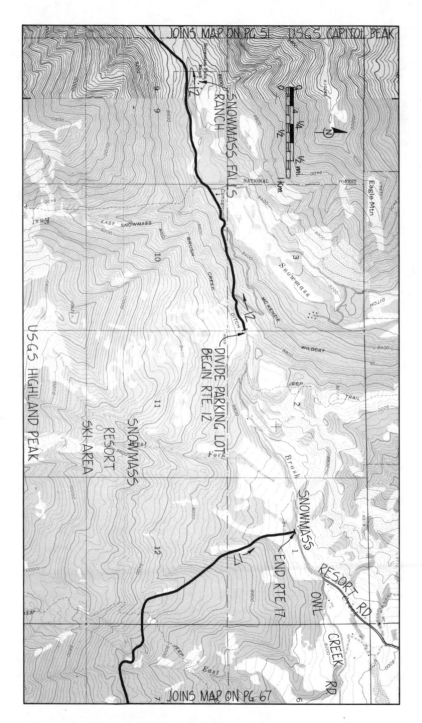

SNOWMASS FALLS RANCH

NATIONAL   FOREST

Eagle Mtn

EAST SNOWMASS

BRUSH   CREEK

Snowmass

McKENZIE

DITCH

WILDCAT

DIVIDE PARKING LOT
BEGIN RTE. 12

JEEP   TRAIL

U.S.G.S. HIGHLAND PEAK

SNOWMASS
RESORT
SKI AREA

Brush

SNOWMASS

END RTE. 17

RESORT RD.

OWL

CREEK RD.

JEEP

East

Pierre Lakes Basin. (Richard Compton photo)

Snowmass Campground from the ski lift loading station on the valley floor.

Once you are out of the ski area, you will end up on the well-traveled, snow-covered road that leads to the Snowmass Falls Ranch. Ski up the valley past the ranch to the point where the USGS *Capitol Peak* map shows the West Snowmass Creek Trail leaving the main Snowmass Creek Trail, crossing Snowmass Creek, and heading up the steep, narrow valley to Moon Lake. Moon Lake is the upper lake on the east side of Daly Pass (the pass between Mount Daly and Capitol Peak).

Find a good way across Snowmass Creek, then double-check your map and be sure that your route up through the aspen forest will allow you to take the marked trail (on the USGS map) across the first ravine (12-A). It is important to find this trail cut, since any other route across the ravine involves unpleasant bushwhacking.

After crossing the ravine, the route follows the right side of the valley for a short distance, then switches to the left side for a final leg up to a nice flat area about ¼ mile below Moon Lake (12-B), where the best camping is. By staying on the left side of the valley for the final part of the route, you avoid an avalanche-prone headwall (12-C) and a nightmarish maze of steep gullies and tangled underbrush.

One of the best things about West Snowmass Creek is the ski back down. If the route is carefully chosen and conditions are good, it is possible to ski the valley almost as if it were a ski area. While you are in the valley, keep your ears open for coyote song.

Avalanche notes: The proper route does not pass over any fracture zones, but it does cross through some runouts, so travel this route during times of lesser hazard. Remember that you will have to ski up to the Divide parking lot on your return.

13   Pierre Lakes Traverse

Difficulty: Advanced
Time: Several days, depending on egress
Distance: 12 miles
Elevation gain: 6,000 feet
Starting elevation: Moon Lake, 11,720 feet
USGS 7.5 minute maps: Capitol Peak, Snowmass Mountain

Map—page 51

The least accessible and most spectacular of the Elk Mountain valleys is the Pierre Lakes Basin between Capitol and Snowmass Peaks. This spring season high-traverse route will bring you into intimate contact with the beautiful basin and its surrounding peaks.

From Moon Lake (see Route 12), climb south to the col (13-A) between Capitol and Clark peaks, taking care to skirt avalanche runouts from the north ridge of Capitol. Once at the col you will see an obvious notch in the rock ridge. Pass through the notch and descend a steep gully to the uppermost Pierre Lake. You must remove your skis to climb through the notch, and it is unlikely that the upper part of the gully will be skiable. The lower portion of the gully opens out onto the broad upper slopes of the basin. The gully itself is relatively protected from avalanches from above, but the slope below is exposed to slides tumbling over the cliffs from the summit slopes of Clark and Capitol. Plan your trip so that you pass through this section early in the day.

From Pierre Basin, ski to Heckert Pass (13-B), which is reached by a long descending traverse around the west side of the basin, then a climb up a narrow, steep-sided valley to the final headwall below the pass. Take the headwall fairly directly to the pass summit. Descend the gully on the south side of the pass all the way to Snowmass Lake. This gully is also avalanche-prone, and should only be skied early in the morning.

From Snowmass Lake, ski out Snowmass Creek (see Route 15).

Avalanche notes: This route should be traveled in spring conditions, with care to be out of avalanche areas when the sun begins to affect the snow.

14   Owl Creek Trail

Difficulty: Novice
Time: 2 hours
Distance: Approximately 3 miles
Elevation gain: Varies with exact route
Starting elevation: Approximately 8,100 feet
USGS 7.5 minute maps: Highland Peak, Aspen

Map—page 67

The Aspen Nordic Council maintains this trail between Snowmass Resort (see Route 12) and Buttermilk Ski Area (see Route 17). It follows a hilly route between and parallel to the Owl Creek Road and the Government Trail. The trail lies mostly on private land crossed by easement; stay on the trail to keep the landowners happy. The trail is well marked and set with a mechanical track setter—once you're on it, you can't miss it! Don't use anything heavier than light touring gear for this one.

To ski the Owl Creek Trail from Snowmass Resort drive to the Snowmass Touring Center. Find the touring center by driving the Snowmass Resort Road to its intersection with the Highline Road at the east end of the golf course (there are X-C ski tracks on the golf course). Drive Highline Road a short way and turn west on Snowmass Club Road. Follow Snowmass Club Road to the touring center on the left just past the Snowmass Club. Inquire at the center for up-to-date trail access.

To ski the Owl Creek Trail from Buttermilk Ski Area drive the West Buttermilk Road (see Route 17) to a well-signed trailhead about a mile before the West Buttermilk parking area. There is parking on the side of the road at the trailhead.

An avalanche in action at Snowmass Resort. (Michael Kennedy photo)

An excellent brochure describing the X-C ski track system in the Roaring Fork Valley is available from the Aspen Nordic Council (see Appendix C).

Avalanche notes: There is virtually no avalanche danger on the trail. Certain hillsides could develop small sluffs in rare conditions.

15   Snowmass Creek to Snowmass Lake

Difficulty: Advanced
Time: 2 days up, 8 hours back
Distance: 9 miles from the Divide parking lot
Elevation gain: 3,000 feet
Starting elevation: 8,920 feet
USGS 7.5 minute maps: Snowmass Mountain, Capitol Peak

Map—page 51

If one had to judge among all the lakes in the Elks for their beauty, Snowmass Lake would take first prize. The almost-mile-long lake leads the way to an enormous snow bowl beneath several 14,000-foot peaks. The panorama of alpine terrain is equal to that usually only experienced from a mountaintop. If you have the inclination to enjoy a true winter wilderness, seriously consider this tour.

From the Divide parking lot (see Route 12), begin the ski up Snowmass Creek. The winter route up the creek stays on the trail as marked on the USGS *Highland Peak* map for about six miles past the Snowmass Falls Ranch. At the six-mile point, near a small oxbow lake (15-A), it is necessary to follow the east side of the valley to avoid the runouts of some huge avalanche slopes on the right. About ¼ mile past the oxbow lake, a dense forest fills the valley. Use the edge of this forest as a safe route to cross back to the west side of the valley. Here the summer trail switchbacks up a huge east-facing avalanche slope (15-B). Do not venture onto this slope. Stay in the trees to the left and climb to where the summer trail enters the woods. Take care to intersect and use the summer trail from here to the lake; otherwise you will have to struggle through dense timber.

Avalanche notes: The portion of the route with the most

SNOWMASS LAKE

SNOWMASS MOUNTAIN

AREA OF
PIERRE LAKES TRAVERSE
(ROUTE 13)

A portion of the Pierre Lakes Traverse can be seen to the right of Snowmass Mountain. (Michael Kennedy photo)

hazard is the narrow section of the valley just before the oxbow lake. Unfortunately, this area is threatened from both sides. It is not the place to be during or just after a snowstorm, nor is it a good camping spot. The route crosses no areas where a skier can actually trigger a slide; the worry is from natural releases. This area is popular for spring skiing when the hazard is more predictable.

16 Snowmass Mountain Summit

Difficulty: Advanced in winter, intermediate in spring
Time: 6 hours round trip
Distance: 4 ½ miles round trip
Elevation gain: 3,000 feet
Starting elevation: 10,980 feet
USGS 7.5 minute map: Snowmass Mountain

Map—page 51

This is probably the most classic ski descent in the Elks. It is seldom done in the winter because of avalanche danger in the huge bowl, but many parties make the trip in the spring.

Climbing the peak is simple. Start from the west end of Snowmass Lake (see Route 15) and climb up the snow bowl to the obvious shoulder (16-A) left (south) of the summit. Be sure you are headed toward the correct peak—it does not look high enough! From the shoulder, follow the rocky ridge to the summit. Most people ski the bowl from the point on the summit ridge gained from the shoulder. For a ski descent from the summit, ski the short north face into the bowl. The first three hundred feet of the face could be classified as extreme skiing, then the angle eases off.

Avalanche notes: The main obstacle to a winter ascent of Snowmass Mountain is safely negotiating the avalanche-prone headwall that leads from the west end of the lake up into the lower-angled portion of the bowl. An astute evaluation of snow stability is necessary to make a decision about the ascent, as there is no safe line up the headwall. Because of this problem the peak has only been climbed several times in the winter.

Skiing on Richmond Hill, with Hayden Peak in the background. (Michael Kennedy photo)

CHAPTER FOUR

The Aspen Area

There are quite a few ski mountaineering trips that begin near the town of Aspen. Because many of them start at the same trailhead or off the same road, they have been grouped accordingly. Driving directions to each group of trailheads are given only once, at the beginning of that section.

Because the trailheads near Aspen are heavily used, you should take care when you park not to block snowplow access or local drivers. If you have any doubts about parking once you are at a

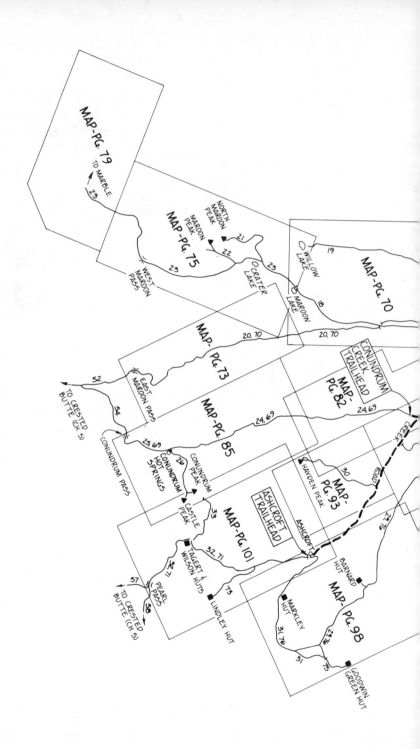

MAP-PG. 79

TO MARBLE
23

NORTH MAROON PEAK
MAROON PEAK
MAP-PG. 75
21
22
23
CRATER LAKE
WEST MAROON PASS
23

WILLOW LAKE
19
MAP-PG. 70
MAROON LAKE
18
20, 70

20, 70

MAP-PG. 73
EAST MAROON PASS
52
54
TO CRESTED BUTTE (CH 5)
CONUNDRUM PASS
25, 69
CONUNDRUM HOT SPRINGS
26
CONUNDRUM PEAK
MAP-PG. 85
24, 69

CONUNDRUM CREEK TRAILHEAD
MAP-PG. 82
24, 69

CREEK

CASTLE PEAK
33
MAP-PG. 101
ASHCROFT TRAILHEAD
HAYDEN PEAK
30
MAP-PG. 93
ROAD
27, 74
ASHCROFT

TAGERT & WILSON HUTS
32, 71
34, 71
PEARL PASS
57
56
TO CRESTED BUTTE (CH 5)
73
LINDLEY HUT
BARNARD HUT
MARKLEY HUT
MAP-PG. 98
31, 76
27, 76
51
75
GOODWIN GREEN HUT

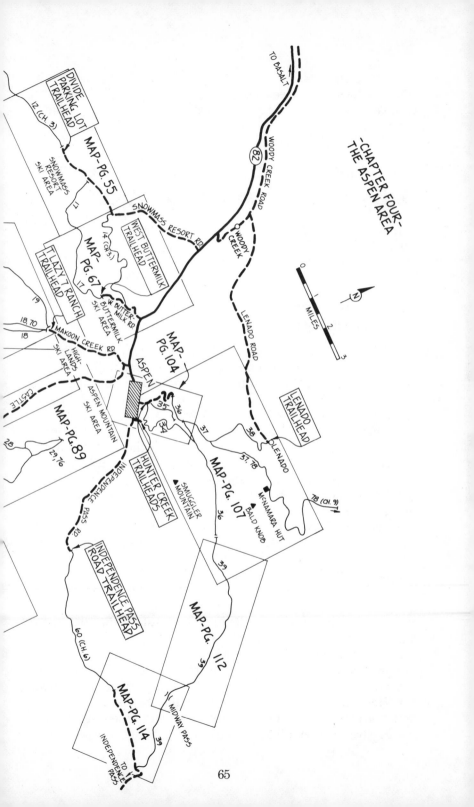

-CHAPTER FOUR-
THE ASPEN AREA

TO BASALT

82

WOODY CREEK ROAD

Woody Creek

LENADO ROAD

MILES
0 1 2 3

N

DIVIDE PARKING LOT TRAILHEAD

12 (CH. 3)

MAP-PG. 55

SNOWMASS RESORT SKI AREA

11

SNOWMASS RESORT RD.

WEST BUTTERMILK TRAILHEAD

14 (CH. 3)

17

MAP-PG. 67

FT LAZY 7 RANCH TRAILHEAD

19

18, 70

18

MAKOON CREEK RD.

W. BUTTERMILK SKI AREA

W. BUTTERMILK RD.

HIGHLANDS SKI AREA

ASPEN

MAP-PG. 104

LENADO TRAILHEAD

LENADO

35   36

34

37

38

37, 78

78 (CH. 9)

CASTLE

MAP-PG. 89

20

29, 76

ASPEN MOUNTAIN SKI AREA

INDEPENDENCE PASS RD.

HUNTER CREEK TRAILHEADS

SMUGGLER MOUNTAIN

MCNAMARA HUT

BALD KNOB

MAP-PG. 107

36

36

INDEPENDENCE PASS ROAD TRAILHEAD

39

60 (CH. 6)

MAP-PG. 112

39

39

MIDWAY PASS

MAP-PG. 114

39

TO INDEPENDENCE PASS

65

roadhead, ask for information from the people living nearby. If this is not possible, at least leave a note on your vehicle explaining its abandonment. If you are planning a trip of several days, make doubly sure you are parked properly.

17 Government Trail from Buttermilk Ski Area to Snowmass Ski Area

Difficulty: Novice
Time: 5 hours
Distance: 5 ½ miles
Elevation gain: Negligible
Starting elevation: 8,400 feet
USGS 7.5 minute maps: Aspen, Highland Peak

Maps—pages 55 and 67

This trail is so named because of the Forest Service's establishment of the trail and its intermittent attempts to maintain and sign it. As it is, the trailheads are not signed and are difficult for the newcomer to locate, but the excellent touring provided by this route is worth the effort it takes to find the trail.

Begin the trip by driving down Highway 82 from Aspen several miles to the Buttermilk Ski Area. Drive past the condominiums and take a left into the obvious Buttermilk Mountain parking area. Once in the parking area, bear right and drive into the utility parking area where you will see many buses and service vehicles parked. From the far southwest corner of this parking area (next to the garages), drive up the steep West Buttermilk Road for about three miles to the West Buttermilk parking area near the ski-lift loading station for West Buttermilk.

From the West Buttermilk parking area, ski a cat track a few hundred feet up and to the right to a metal gate at the western boundary of the ski area. Cross the gate and follow the road cut through the timber, which will climb in a westerly direction with one short switchback to the left.

In less than a mile you will come to a clearing. Head to the left into the aspen trees and stay on the trail (which is obvious), and you will soon come to a small pond (Whites Lake) with a cabin next to it. Here the trail climbs a bit to the left, then heads in the general direction of Snowmass Resort ski area. After this there are several places where it is tempting to drop down to the north, especially if

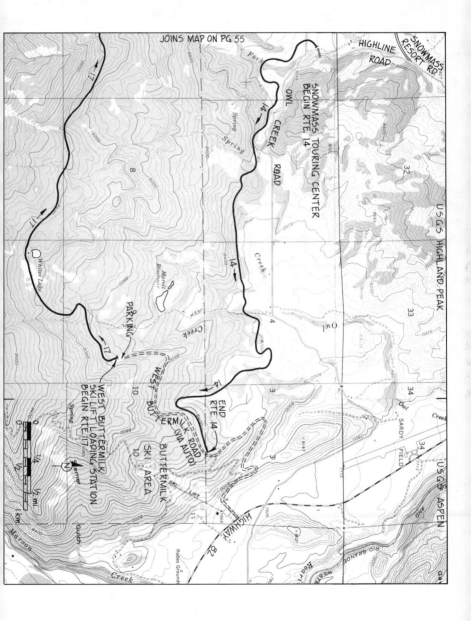

HIGHLINE ROAD

SNOWMASS RESORT RD.

SNOWMASS TOURING CENTER BEGIN RTE. 14

OWL CREEK ROAD

USGS HIGHLAND PEAK

Spring Fork

Spring

14

14

Creek

Marolt Reservoir

Owl

JEEP

Creek

PARKING

14

END RTE. 14

WEST BUTTERMILK

WEST BUTTERMILK SKI LIFT LOADING STATION BEGIN RTE. 17

BUTTERMILK ROAD (VIA AUTO)

BUTTERMILK SKI AREA

SKI LIFT

Spring

Maroon

Gulch

Creek

Rodeo Grounds

HIGHWAY 82

RIO GRANDE ROW

RIO GRANDE ROW (WEST)

SARDY FIELD

USGS ASPEN

Del Creek

White Lake

N

Denver

0
1/4
1/2
1/2 mi
1 km

Ski touring on the Government Trail. (Michael Kennedy photo)

you are slightly confused. Do not make this mistake. Remember that the trail takes only a few short drops the remainder of the way to Snowmass. A helpful note regarding navigation is that the popularity of the Government Trail usually ensures a good set of tracks to follow—but make sure you are not following a two-legged sheep! If you do get lost, follow any drainage down to the north and you will end up on either Owl Creek Road or Snowmass Resort Road.

The trail intersects the eastern boundary of the Snowmass Resort at a point high enough to make possible a good run down the packed slopes. From Snowmass Resort there is a reliable bus service back to Aspen or Buttermilk.

Avalanche notes: In rare conditions there are several grassy hillsides that could be dangerous. A conversation with any ski patrolman or a call to the Forest Service will help you decide if conditions are safe.

18 Maroon Creek Ski Trail and Maroon Creek Road

Difficulty: Novice
Time: 6 hours round trip, either route
Distance: 14 miles round trip
Elevation gain: 1,200 feet
Starting elevation: 8,236 feet
USGS 7.5 minute maps: Highland Peak, Maroon Bells

Map—page 70

The T Lazy 7 Guest Ranch rents snowmobiles in the winter, and the drivers use the unplowed portion of the Maroon Creek Road for their primary route up the valley. Skiers can use their packed trail, but it is a bit nasty with the exhaust, noise, and moguls created by the machines.

An alternative to the road is a trail that follows the other side of Maroon Creek almost all the way to the East Maroon Trail Footbridge (18-A). Find this trail by skiing up the road from the ranch a few hundred feet, then crossing a footbridge down and to the left over Maroon Creek. Once across the creek, the trail travels through a series of open meadows (avalanche runouts) and forests.

Drive west out of Aspen on Highway 82. On your left a short distance out of town you will see the well-signed turnoff to the Castle Creek and Maroon Creek roads. The Aspen Municipal Golf Course will be on your right and the steeple of the Prince of Peace Chapel will be visible to the left. Take the turn and drive up the well-signed Maroon Creek Road. In winter the road is plowed for three miles up to the T Lazy 7 Guest Ranch. In the spring and summer the road is open all the way to Maroon Lake, but then, access is restricted to public bus service at times other than the early morning and late evening. For up-to-date information about the Maroon Creek Road, call the Forest Service in Aspen (see Appendix C).

Avalanche notes: Both routes up the Maroon Creek Valley are threatened by natural releases, the road less so than the trail. Huge slides come down off the Highland Ridge on the east side of the valley, and several of these regularly cross the creek and road. Farther up the valley there are dangerous paths that threaten the road from the southeast side of Sievers Mountain. Unless conditions are fairly stable, avoid skiing anything in this valley other than the first several miles of the road.

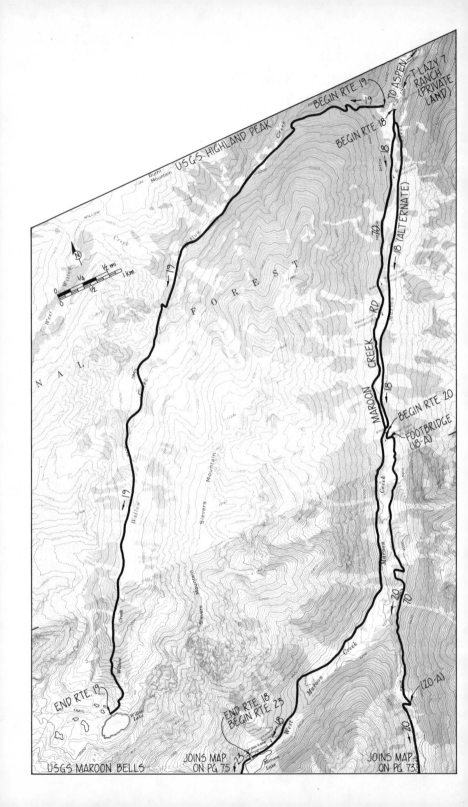

USGS HIGHLAND PEAK

TO ASPEN

T LAZY 7 RANCH (PRIVATE LAND)

BEGIN RTE. 19

19

BEGIN RTE. 18

18

Burnt Mountain

Willow Creek

19

18 (ALTERNATE)

FOREST

NATIONAL

MAROON CREEK RD.

N

½ mi.
¼
0 ½ 1 km.

Willow Creek

19

Sievers Mountain

BEGIN RTE. 20

FOOTBRIDGE (18-A)

18

Maroon Creek

Sievers Mountain

20

70

(20-A)

END RTE. 19

TRAIL

Willow Lake

END RTE. 18
BEGIN RTE. 23

18

23

West Maroon Creek

Maroon Lake

20

USGS MAROON BELLS

JOINS MAP ON PG. 75

JOINS MAP ON PG. 73

19   Willow Creek from T Lazy 7 Guest Ranch

Difficulty: Advanced to the lake; intermediate half way
Time: 16 hours to Willow Lake and back, an easy day tour to the
  halfway point
Distance: 7 miles to the lake
Elevation gain: 3,600 feet to the lake
Starting elevation: 8,236 feet
USGS 7.5 minute maps: Highland Peak, Maroon Bells

Map—page 70

Follow the Maroon Creek Road to the T Lazy 7 Guest Ranch (see Route 18). The Willow Creek Trail takes off to the west up the Willow Creek drainage just south of the T Lazy 7 Guest Ranch. The

Give snowmobiles plenty of room, and remember you won't see them where you're headed. (Lou Dawson photo)

winter route stays fairly close to the trail marked on the USGS maps, with obvious deviations to avoid avalanche runouts from Burnt Mountain, Baldy Mountain, and Sievers Mountain. The route is easy to find and can be skied all the way to Willow Lake, but most parties turn back well before the lake in order to make an enjoyable day trip. You must ask permission at the ranch to cross their private land in order to get into the Willow Creek Valley.

Avalanche notes: Avoid the upper part of the valley during high-risk periods.

20   East Maroon Valley to East Maroon Pass

Difficulty: Advanced
Time: 7 hours from ranch to pass
Distance: 11 miles
Elevation gain: 3,700 feet
Starting elevation: 9,000 feet
USGS 7.5 minute maps: Highland Peak, Maroon Bells

Maps—pages 70 and 73

This is an interesting and fairly safe trip. It forms half of one of the recommended routes connecting Crested Butte and Aspen (see Route 70).

Follow the Maroon Creek Road for about three miles up the valley from the T Lazy 7 Guest Ranch (see Route 18), to where the East Maroon Trail footbridge crosses Maroon Creek to the east (8,709 feet; there is a wilderness portal sign here). Cross the footbridge and follow the obvious trail cut, marked on the USGS *Maroon Bells* map, that leads up the East Maroon Valley. Stay on the trail until it intersects a deep, washed-out gully (20-A) about three miles from the footbridge. Do not try to cross this gully, simply backtrack several hundred feet, then drop down and cross East Maroon Creek. Stay on the west side of the creek until you arrive at the border of the dense spruce forest filling the south end of the valley at 10,200 feet (to arrive at this point you will pass through several other smaller forests).

At the big forest it is necessary to cross the creek again and find the old mule trail cut through the forest on the east side of the valley (this is the official trail on the USGS *Maroon Bells* map). If you miss the trail, there is a desperate bushwhack ahead.

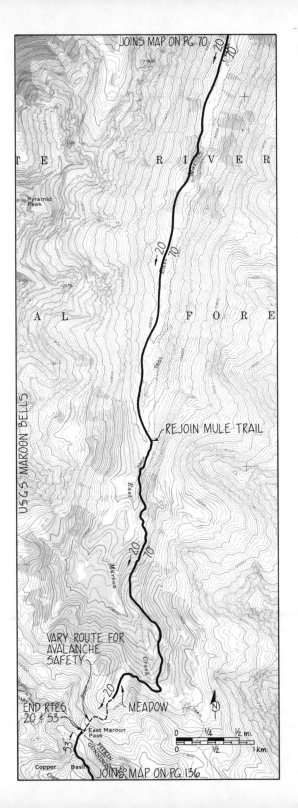

JOINS MAP ON PG. 70

20
70

Pyramid
Peak

20
70

TE   R I V E R

A L   F O R E

USGS MAROON BELLS

REJOIN MULE TRAIL

East

20
70

Maroon

VARY ROUTE FOR
AVALANCHE
SAFETY

20

MEADOW

END RTES
20 & 53

East Maroon
Pass

N

53

PITKIN

GUNNISON

Creek

Trail

Copper

Basin

0   ¼   ½ mi.

0   ½   1 km.

JOINS MAP ON PG. 136

The old mule trail follows a gradually climbing contour around the east side of the valley, eventually leading to the marshy meadow shown on the map and just below the pass (still the official trail marked on the map). At the meadow, leave the trail on the USGS map and head up and slightly left, using some small stands of trees and several ribs to form a route up to the pass that will be safer from avalanches. This deviation is important, as the official trail cuts across several major avalanche paths. From the pass, reverse the above route. Or follow Routes 51, 52, and 53 to Crested Butte (see Route 70).

Avalanche notes: The first part of the East Maroon Trail is threatened by some massive avalanches off Highlands Ridge. This dangerous area can be avoided by starting up the East Maroon Valley at the point where East Maroon Creek enters Maroon Creek. The remainder of the trail regularly crosses avalanche runouts.

21 North Face of North Maroon Peak

Difficulty: Extreme
Time: 4 ½ hours from a high camp in the bowl below the face
Distance: 5 miles from Maroon Lake
Elevation gain: 4,000 feet
Starting elevation: 9,580 feet
USGS 7.5 minute map: Maroon Bells

Map—page 75

The north face of North Maroon Peak provides the most classic extreme ski descent in the Elks. The descent was first done by Fritz Stammberger in spring of 1971. In those days few people had even considered extreme skiing in Colorado. Stammberger's feat changed that and kindled a spate of ski descents.

After Stammberger's, the most radical descent of the face was that of Ted Miners. He slipped while negotiating the tricky traverse onto the lower snow field, and was launched into the air over the lower headwall for a ride that included several hundred feet of flight time. He survived because of a gradual runout on the steep snow at the base of the cliff. The lower headwall has been dubbed "Ted Miners' Memorial Ski Jump" to honor his feat.

Drive the Maroon Creek Road to Maroon Lake (see Route 18). As with all extreme ski descents, it is best to climb the peak via the ski

USGS MAROON BELLS

MAROON LAKE

END RTE 18
BEGIN RTE 23

18

BEGIN RTE 21

(21A)

Minnehaha   TRAIL

Gulch

21

Sleeping

Sexton

END RTE 21

BEGIN RTE 22

22

SKIABLE STEEP
GULLIES—
END RTE 22

Fravert

Basin

POSSIBLE
AVALANCHE SLOPE

USGS SNOWMASS MTN.

WHITE

NATION

ELK

23

Pyramid Peak and Maroon Bells. (Lou Dawson photo)

route. To accomplish this, follow tne West Maroon Pass Trail from Maroon Lake (Route 23) up the valley to its intersection with the Buckskin Pass Trail a short distance before Crater Lake. Follow the Buckskin Trail to the 11,000-foot level. Leave the trail here (21-A) and cross Minnehaha Creek, then traverse up and left along some prominent shelves that lead to the snowbowl below the north face.

Observed from the snowbowl, the face has two obvious features. They are the Miners' Ski Jump and the long snowfield that stretches across the face above the jump. Above the snowfield the face is a jumble of snow patches and rock outcroppings. The features in the middle of the face form a steep gully system broken by several rock bands. This is the central gully.

Crampons and an ice axe are essential for the climb, and many people have used a rope for parts of both ascent and descent.

Begin the climb up the north face by hiking up the snowbowl to the right side of the face. From here it is easy to climb up to the long snowfield mentioned above (there may be a bergschrund to cross).

Traverse the snowfield to the left until you are below the central gully. The route heads up the gully and becomes slightly devious. If you run into problems here remember that, due to the horizontal stratification of the rock, a short traverse will lead around most obstacles.

At the top of the central gully the route becomes easy. You will arrive at a second large snowfield topped by another broken rock band. There are several ways through this band, usually a bit to the right. After this rock band you will come to a third snowfield topped by a more forbidding, less broken rock band, called "The Punk Rock Band," which has stymied many parties. Avoid it by traversing to the left and climbing the last portion of the easy northeast ridge route. Classified as "extreme," this route is dangerous and should be attempted only by *experienced* extreme skiers.

Stammberger is the only person to have skied directly off the summit to the face. To accomplish this he had to fall over the Punk Rock Band. All subsequent descents have been made by climbing down the Northeast Ridge to the point where it is possible to ski out onto the snowfield under the upper cliff band. From here follow your ascent route. The crux of the descent usually is negotiating steep skiing in the central gully.

Avalanche notes: Attempt this route only early in the morning on consolidated spring snow.

22   South Maroon Gullies

Difficulty: Extreme
Time: 4 ½ hours from a high camp at Crater Lake
Distance: 2 miles one way from Crater Lake
Elevation gain: 4,000 feet
Starting elevation: 10,076 feet
USGS 7.5 minute map: Maroon Bells

Map—page 75

On the east side of South Maroon Peak, to the south of the summit and facing Crater Lake, are two excellent ski gullies. They are borderline extreme skiing: not as dangerous as North Maroon (Route 21), yet serious enough to require an ice axe and crampons for the ascent. Early in the spring it is possible to make a run from near the summit of South Maroon Peak down one of the gullies, then all the way to the valley floor. Unfortunately, the snow on the lower portion of the route melts quickly, and consequently most parties do their skiing above the 11,000-foot level and end by hiking down the lower portion. Another factor to consider when planning this trip is that in the late spring, deep channels form in the snow in the lower parts of the gullies. These channels become too deep and narrow to ski.

Drive the Maroon Creek Road to Maroon Lake (see Route 18). Climb to the gullies from a point on the West Maroon Trail (Route 23) about ¾ of a mile past Crater Lake. The route is simple and obvious.

Avalanche notes: This is another route that should be skied only after the spring snow consolidation.

23 West Maroon Valley to Schofield Park via West Maroon Pass

Difficulty: Advanced
Time: 2 days to Schofield Park with another 1 or 2 to regain civilization
Distance: 17 miles to the park
Elevation gain: 4,000 feet
Starting elevation: 9,580 feet
USGS 7.5 minute maps: Maroon Bells, Snowmass Mountain, Oh-Be-Joyful, Gothic, Marble

Maps—pages 75 and 79

This is one of the longer tours in the Elks. *It is not a safe route in the winter* because of the wind-loaded avalanche slope that forms the final ascent on the east side of the pass. In early spring, however, this is a perfect trip because of the consistently high elevation.

Most of the route is obvious, though a bit of map reading is necessary for first-timers. Follow the Maroon Creek Road to Maroon Lake (see Route 18). From the lake, take the trail, as marked on the USGS *Maroon Bells* map, up to Crater Lake and then on up the valley to the pass. After climbing over the pass you will have a bit of steep skiing on the west side. But most of the terrain down the East Fork drainage to Schofield Park is a relaxing cruise. The park is a beautiful place to camp, and there is a

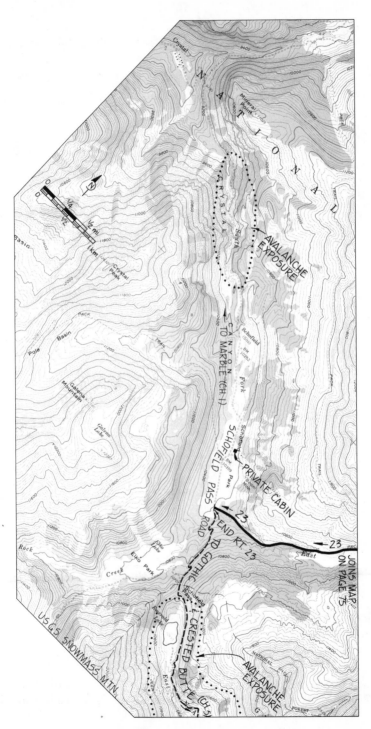

Skiing near Hayden Peak. (Michael Kennedy photo)

dilapidated private cabin that is open to the public and can be used in a pinch. To return to civilization, either retrace your route from Maroon Lake or follow the Schofield Pass Road south to Gothic or north to Marble (see Chapter 1). Both these destinations are close to main roads.

Avalanche notes: For the best and safest skiing, this route should be done during a stable period in early spring. You may want to make some deviations to avoid avalanche runouts from Maroon Bells and Pyramid Peak. The Emerald Lake section on the way to Gothic and the Punchbowl section on the way to Marble are both hazardous and are not recommended except during the most stable times.

24 Conundrum Hot Springs from Castle Creek Road

Difficulty: Advanced
Time: 10 hours one way
Distance: 9 miles one way
Elevation gain: 2,700 feet
Starting elevation: 8,600 feet
USGS 7.5 minute maps: Maroon Bells, Hayden Peak, Aspen

Maps—pages 82 and 85

For many years skiers who ventured into the Conundrum Creek Valley were looked upon as crazy fools. Perhaps this attitude was a result of the Forest Service description of the valley as the most avalanche prone in the Elk Mountains. It is true that the valley is riddled with avalanche paths, but in most conditions there is a reasonably safe route up the valley to the hot springs.

This is a difficult trip, and quite a few skiers have been rescued from the valley. There have never been any avalanche accidents in Conundrum, however, and this good record can continue if skiers take standard precautions and stick to the following route. This trail avoids crossing any avalanche trigger areas, and exposes the skier to a minimum of runout zones.

Drive west out of Aspen on Highway 82. A short way out of town you will see the well-signed turnoff to Castle Creek and Maroon Creek. The Aspen Municipal Golf Course will be on your right and the steeple of the Prince of Peace Chapel will be visible to the left. At this turnoff from Highway 82, take a hard left onto the Castle Creek Road, the left of the two forks (the right is the Maroon Creek Road). The road is well signed.

Drive five miles up the Castle Creek Road. At this point the poorly signed Conundrum Creek Road (the only sign says "Restricted Bridge") heads down to the right, crosses Castle Creek, then heads up the Conundrum Valley. Follow the Conundrum Creek Road about a mile to a snowplow turnaround. There is no parking here, so have someone drop you off, or park on the Castle Creek Road.

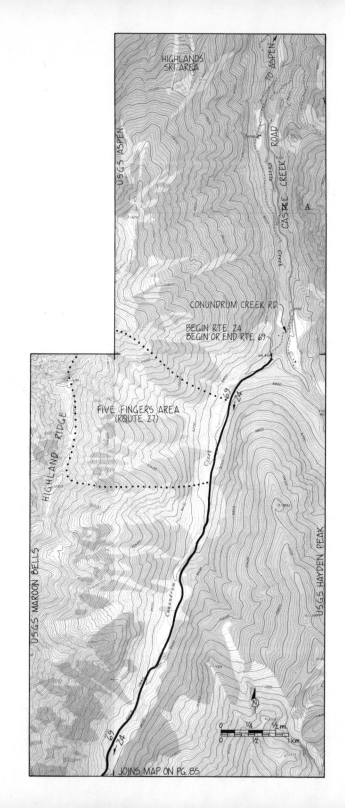

HIGHLANDS
SKI AREA

TO ASPEN

U.S.G.S ASPEN

CASTLE CREEK ROAD

Castle Creek

A

CONUNDRUM CREEK RD

BEGIN RTE 24
BEGIN OR END RTE. 69

FIVE FINGERS AREA
(ROUTE 27)

HIGHLAND RIDGE

Conundrum Creek

U.S.G.S MAROON BELLS

U.S.G.S HAYDEN PEAK

69
24

N

0   1/4   1/2 mi.

0   1/2   1 km

JOINS MAP ON PG. 85

From the plow turnaround, ski up the Conundrum Creek trail-road as it is marked on the USGS *Hayden Peak* map. In the first few miles you will cross several open areas that are threatened by avalanche chutes on the west side of the valley. *Give the runouts of these chutes a wide berth.* Continue up the valley to the point where the trail marked on the USGS *Hayden Peak* map crosses to the USGS *Maroon Bells* map. This point is easy to spot while traveling because the valley rapidly becomes narrow and more heavily timbered.

At this narrowing point, leave the trail marked on the USGS map and bushwhack directly up the valley, with the creek on your left. Cross the creek where a steep hillside blocks the way on the right (24-A), this point is the beginning of the narrow gorge shown on the USGS *Maroon Bells* map beginning at the 9,720-foot level.

Stay out of the gorge by skiing the left side of Conundrum Creek for about a quarter-mile past Cataract Creek, then heading up and left (24-B) to follow a route through some sparse timber that will gain the large open shelf (24-C) that is shown on the USGS *Maroon Bells* map just north of the word "creek." Continue up the valley by skiing along this shelf to its southern end, then crossing the creek and intersecting the trail marked on the map. While skiing the shelf, be aware of the avalanche paths on the east side of the valley.

Stay on the summer trail marked on the USGS *Maroon Bells* map the remainder of the way to the springs. It is difficult to find where the summer trail is cut through several stands of dense timber in the upper portion of the valley. Persevere at these places, and take time to read the map—a lost skier can encounter impassable underbrush. For those with the wherewithal to ski to Conundrum Hot Springs, the reward is worth the effort. The pool is the perfect temperature for a lengthy stay, and the view is hard to beat. It is a unique place and a privilege to enjoy without the summer's hordes.

When you reach the edge of the springs you will be confronted by a dilemma foreign to most winter mountaineering: how, while standing in a subzero breeze, do you remove layer upon layer of clothing, take a bath, climb out of the water dripping wet, then get dressed without freezing into one of Medusa's statues? The most effective immersion technique begins with the careful arrange-ment of your clothes, so that you can dress as rapidly as possible when you leave the pool. In a more serious vein, do be careful of hypothermia while exiting the pool.

The worst mistake you can make is to succumb to temptation, stay in the pool until after dark, and not have a lamp handy. It is easy to imagine the consequences of this kind of poor planning. Once a man from Aspen actually skied to the springs totally nude (no gear except skis and a hat), spent the night in the pool, then skied back to civilization the next morning! There are stories of others who tried this and were stormed in at the springs for days—it is said they were genetically altered, and started a race of sentient prunes.

Avalanche notes: The route described above avoids crossing some dangerous avalanche slopes on the west side of the valley. Even so, constant care must be taken to recognize and skirt many avalanche runout zones. This is one of the most complex valley routes in the Elks.

25 Conundrum Hot Springs to Conundrum Pass

Difficulty: Advanced
Time: 4 hours
Distance: 2 miles from the springs
Elevation gain: 1,600 feet
Starting elevation: 11,200 feet
USGS 7.5 minute maps: Maroon Bells, Gothic

Map—page 85

This route allows a beautiful view of the Elk Range and some good skiing in Conundrum Basin.

Please note that on the USGS *Gothic* quadrangle map, Conundrum Pass is marked as Triangle Pass; on the USGS *Maroon Bells* map (1960) disregard what is marked as Conundrum Pass. Drive the Castle Creek Road (see Route 24) to the Conundrum Creek Road trailhead. Follow Route 24 to Conundrum Hot Springs. The route is simple: from the springs, ski directly south up a small hill into Conundrum Basin. From the midpart of the basin, follow a series of ribs and shelves for a route that is reasonably safe from avalanches to the pass. Return is via the same route.

Avalanche notes: The slope on this route that slides most frequently is the small bowl on the east side of Conundrum Pass (just below the saddle). This slope can be avoided by traveling on either of the wind-scoured rocky ribs forming the sides of the bowl.

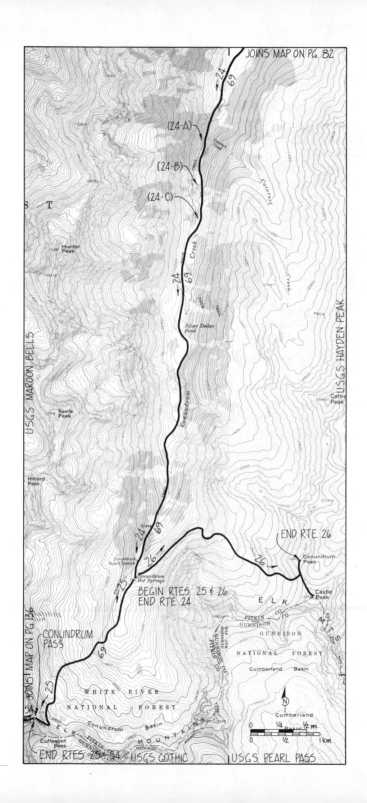

JOINS MAP ON PG. 82

24
69

(24-A)

(24-B)

(24-C)

USGS MAROON BELLS

Hunter Peak

Keefe Peak

Hilliard Peak

24
69

Silver Dollar Pond

Conundrum Creek

USGS HAYDEN PEAK

Cataract Creek

Cathe Peak

END RTE. 26

26

Conundrum Peak

24
69

26

Conundrum Guard Station

Conundrum Hot Springs

BEGIN RTES. 25 & 26
END RTE. 24

Castle Peak

ELK

PITKIN CO.
GUNNISON CO.

GUNNISON

NATIONAL   FOREST

Cumberland   Basin

M T S

CONUNDRUM PASS

69

25

JOINS MAP ON PG. 136

WHITE   RIVER

NATIONAL   FOREST

Conundrum   Basin

ELK   MOUNTAINS

N

Cumberland Basin

0   ¼   ½ mi.

0   ½   1 km

Coffeepot Pass

END RTES. 25 & 24   USGS GOTHIC   USGS PEARL PASS

26   Conundrum Hot Springs to Castle Peak and Conundrum Peak

Difficulty: Advanced
Time: 8 hours round trip from Conundrum Springs
Distance: 3 miles
Elevation gain: 3,000 feet
Starting elevation: 11,200 feet
USGS 7.5 minute maps: Maroon Bells, Hayden Peak

Map—page 85

This is one of the easier (though still serious) winter "fourteener" climbs in the Elks. Drive the Castle Creek Road (see Route 24) to the Conundrum Creek Road trailhead. Follow Route 24 to Conundrum Hot Springs. From the springs, contour back to the northeast along the east side of the valley and into the enormous basin below Castle and Conundrum peaks. Follow the basin up to the saddle between the peaks, then follow the obvious ridges to either summit. Return by the same route or by Montezuma Basin (Route 33) if avalanche conditions are extremely safe.

Avalanche notes: Much of this route crosses over possible avalanche slopes. Due to high winds, which are common on this side of the peaks, there are many days in winter when a safe route can be found on wind-scoured and compacted snow. The skiing at these times may not be ideal, but the summits are worth the trip. Spring, of course, is a wonderful time for a climb and ski descent of these peaks.

27   Spring Skiing off Highland Ridge

Difficulty: Advanced
Time: 6 hours
Distance: 2 miles direct; 6 miles via ski area
Elevation gain: 3,000 feet
Starting elevation: 8,600 feet
USGS 7.5 minute maps: Maroon Bells, Hayden Peak, Highland Peak, Aspen

Map—page 82

The west side of the Conundrum Creek Valley is formed by the beautiful Highland Ridge. In the spring there is some excellent

Highland Peak is on the right, and Highland Ridge extends to the left. Spring skiing routes drop down the obvious chutes into the Conundrum Creek Valley. (Lou Dawson photo)

and very accessible skiing down the wide gullies that drop into Conundrum from various points along the ridge for about a mile past Highland Peak. These gullies are called "The Five Fingers." Drive the Castle Creek Road (see Route 24) to the Conundrum Creek Road trailhead. Follow Route 24 up the Conundrum Creek Valley to the bottom of the gullies. From there, hike directly up the gullies. An alternative for access is to drive up the Maroon Creek (Route 18) road to the Highlands Ski Area. Then hike up the ski area and out along the ridge to the gullies. You will need permission to hike up the ski area since part of it is on private land.

Avalanche notes: Take normal precautions and ski during a spring morning when the snow is still frozen.

Skiing in the Little Annie area, with Hayden Peak in the background. (Lou Dawson photo)

28   Little Annie Road to Richmond Hill

Difficulty: Intermediate
Time: 4 hours to the ridgetop
Distance: 4 miles
Elevation gain: 1,800 feet
Starting elevation: 8,880 feet
USGS 7.5 minute maps: Hayden Peak, Aspen

Map—page 89

This is an interesting, scenic tour that provides access to excellent low-angle downhill skiing terrain and several other routes. To do this tour, follow the Castle Creek Road (see Route 24) for seven miles to the unsigned Little Annie Road, which turns off to the left (east). Though the turnoff is a bit obscure, there are no

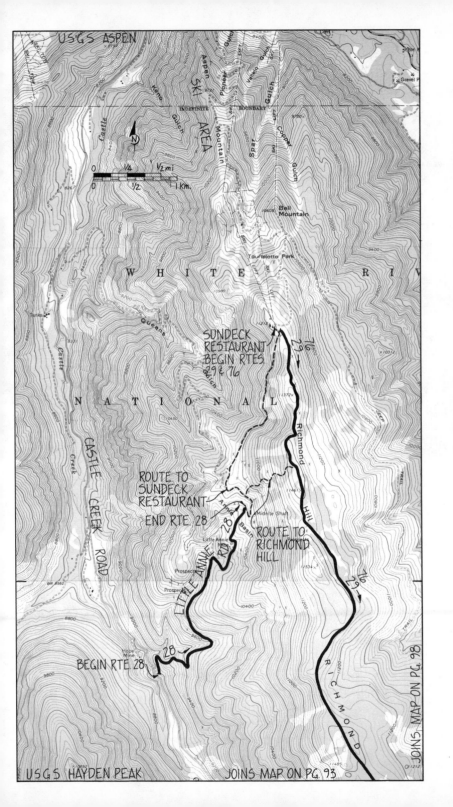

SKI AREA

INDEFINITE BOUNDARY

N

0   ¼   ½ mi
0   ½   1 Km.

Bell Mountain

Tourtelotte Park

W H I T E   R I V

N A T I O N A L

Queens

CASTLE CREEK ROAD

Castle Creek

SUNDECK
RESTAURANT
BEGIN RTES.
29 & 76

76
29

Richmond Hill

Deer

ROUTE TO
SUNDECK
RESTAURANT

END RTE. 28

Midnite Shaft

ROUTE TO
RICHMOND
HILL

Little Annie Mine

Annie Basin

LITTLE ANNIE RD. 28

Prospector

Prospect

76
29

BEGIN RTE. 28

Hope Mine

28

RICHMOND

JOINS MAP ON PG. 98

One of the old cabins in Little Annie Basin. Highland Ridge is in the distance. (Lou Dawson photo)

others at this point. The road is plowed a ways up, but there is no parking—park on the Castle Creek Road.

Ski or walk up the plowed portion of the road, then stay on the snow-covered road (it will probably be packed by ski-doo or snow-cat) as it winds its way up to Little Annie Basin, a large open area with obvious downhill skiing terrain and several cabins. Once in the basin, either switchback up through the trees to the crest of Richmond Hill, or follow the road shown on the USGS *Aspen* map that leads to the top of the Aspen Mountain Ski Area. To return, either follow Richmond Hill to the south (see Route 29), or head down the ski area to Aspen, or ski the terrain in the basin and return to Castle Creek via the ascent route.

Avalanche notes: Most of this route has no avalanche danger. The open slopes in the basin slide on rare occasions.

29 Richmond Hill

Difficulty: Novice to advanced
Time: 5 hours, depending on route
Distance: 4 miles, depending on route
Elevation gain: Depends on route
Starting elevation: 11,212 feet
USGS 7.5 minute maps: Aspen, Hayden Peak, New York Peak

Maps—pages 89 and 98

The ridge behind Aspen Mountain Ski Area, separating the Castle Creek drainage from the upper Roaring Fork drainage, is called Richmond Hill. The area is very scenic and provides a great deal of excellent touring of varied difficulty.

Richmond Hill can be reached several ways. Either hike or ride the lifts up the Aspen Mountain Ski Area, or ski the Little Annie Tour (see Route 28).

Once on the ridge you will have good novice travel for about four miles to the south. Then the route-finding becomes more difficult (29-A). The ridge eventually leads to the east side of Ashcroft Mountain and the Gold Hill area (see Routes 31, 75, 76). A good extended trip combines a tour along Richmond Hill with the Taylor Pass Road to Ashcroft (see Routes 31 and 76).

Avalanche notes: Most of the terrain on the crest of Richmond Hill is safe, though there are many avalanche paths dropping off into the Castle Creek and Roaring Fork valleys. Beware of occasional cornices. The area is windy, so watch for wind-loading, and use scoured areas for safe routes.

30 Hayden Peak

Difficulty: Advanced
Time: 8 hours
Distance: 4 ½ miles
Elevation gain: 4,300 feet
Starting elevation: 9,000 feet
USGS 7.5 minute map: Hayden Peak

Map—page 93

Hayden Peak is the most popular alpine touring area near Aspen. Most skiing is done off the subsidiary summit north of the main summit. This peak is called Ski Hayden (Point 13,316 on the

Making tracks on Ski Hayden. (Lou Dawson photo)

USGS *Hayden Peak* map). To start the tour, drive up the Castle Creek Road (see Route 24) and park at a slightly widened place almost eight miles from the highway turnoff. If you are in the correct place you will have a good view of the Ski Hayden summit, and will be at the foot of the Sawyer Creek drainage.

The ski ascent route generally follows the Sawyer Creek drainage. At the parking place you will be about an eighth of a mile downstream from the Sawyer Creek-Castle Creek confluence. Ski a short distance down and cross Castle Creek. Head up through a sparse aspen forest until you intersect an obvious road cut through the trees. Follow this road as it leads up the Sawyer Creek drainage, crosses the usually snow-covered creek at the 9,480-foot level, then heads up through a pine forest to a small flat area at the 9,600-foot level (30-A). The obvious road cut ends here. Bear left and find a more obscure trail at the south end of the flat area. This

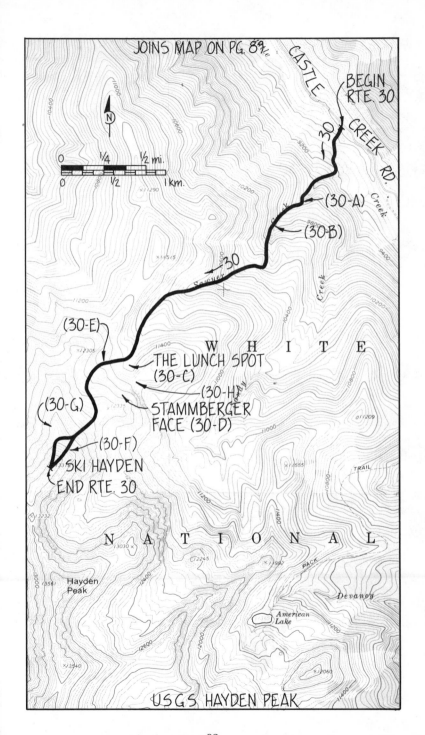

BEGIN
RTE. 30

CASTLE CREEK RD.

30

(30-A)

(30-B)

30

Sawyer

(30-E)

W H I T E

THE LUNCH SPOT
(30-C)

(30-H)

(30-G)

STAMMBERGER
FACE (30-D)

(30-F)

SKI HAYDEN
END RTE. 30

N A T I O N A L

Hayden
Peak

Devaney

American
Lake

TRAIL

PACK

Top: *View south from Bald Knob. The Hayden Peak summits are in the center; Richmond Hill is the long ridge with the sparsely treed areas. (Lou Dawson photo)* Bottom: *Mount Hayden. Ski Hayden is the summit on the right; the true summit is on the left. (Michael Kennedy photo)*

The twin gullies on Ski Hayden. The best ascent route is on the center rib. (Lou Dawson photo)

trail will lead to the base of a narrow gully (30-B). Stay out of the gully by crossing to the right through the trees at the base, then skiing up through the trees with the gully on your left.

At the top of the gully, where the angle eases off, head up and left until you intersect the creek again at approximately the 10,000-foot level. Follow the most logical route up the creek to the large clearing where Sawyer Creek (on the USGS *Hayden Peak* map) begins (30-C), called the Lunch Spot. The steep wall directly ahead, dropping from 12,335 feet (Pokress Point), is the Stammberger Face (30-D). This steep, avalanche-prone headwall was one of Fritz Stammberger's favorite ski descents. It gets skied quite a bit. Fritz Stammberger was a famous local mountaineer who never returned from a solo Himalayan climbing trip. He is well known for his first ski descent of North Maroon Peak (Route 21).

If you turn to the right from the Stammberger Face, you will see a pair of gullies (30-E) that lead up to the Ski Hayden Bowl (see map in text). Follow the sparsely treed rib that separates these gullies, then bear left up the bowl toward the summit. The

Looking up at the Stammberger Face from the Lunch Spot on Ski Hayden. (Lou Dawson photo)

remainder of the route to the summit is either an obvious trudge straight up the northeast face (30-F) or follows a ridge route from the 12,800-foot saddle (30-G). The descent route follows the ascent fairly closely.

The true summit of Hayden Peak can be reached either of two ways: either follow the ridge from Ski Hayden (fairly difficult with dangerous cornices), or ski down the southeast face of Ski Hayden then up the north face of Hayden. The latter route should only be done during a time of very stable avalanche conditions. Return from skiing on Hayden by climbing up to the small saddle (30-H) separating the Sandy Creek drainage from the Lunch Spot. Ski down to the Lunch Spot and return via the Ski Hayden route.

Avalanche notes: A young man was killed by an avalanche in the gully up on the right as you pass through the lower aspen forest. Be very wary of the runout of this gully. There are also several major avalanches in the upper bowl every winter. During periods of moderate to low hazard, the bowl has been skied countless times without mishap. But it can run big and does so at least once a year.

31   Gold Hill Area to or from Ashcroft

Difficulty: Advanced
Time: 7 hours round trip
Distance: 10 miles round trip
Elevation gain: 2,500 feet
Starting elevation: 9,498 feet
USGS 7.5 minute maps: Hayden Peak, New York Peak

Map—page 98

This route combines with the Richmond Hill routes (29, 75, and 76) to form a good extended trip. Navigation in the Gold Hill area is difficult, so be prepared to spend some time orienteering.

Drive the Castle Creek Road (see Route 24) to its winter terminus at the old ghost town of Ashcroft, about 10 miles from the highway junction. Here the Ashcroft Ski Touring Center operates a system of maintained cross-country ski trails that are excellent for the beginner or race-oriented skier. You can pay the required fee for trail use at their office near the road terminus. For people skiing into the mountains, there are several public access corridors through the ski area, one following the snow covered Castle Creek Road (see Route 32), and another cutting across the valley for the

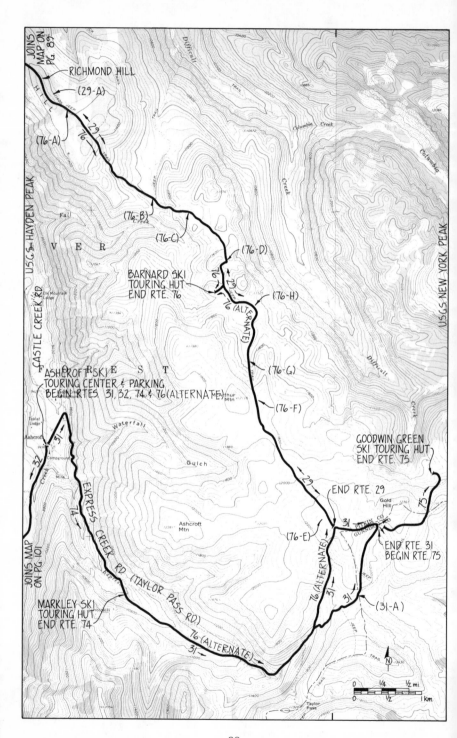

JOINS
MAP ON
PG. 89

RICHMOND HILL
(29-A)

(76-A)

29

76

HILL

U.S.G.S. HAYDEN PEAK

Difficult

Trail

Creek

Columbia Creek

Columbia

U.S.G.S. NEW YORK PEAK

(76-B)
Fall
Creek

(76-C)

(76-D)

BARNARD SKI
TOURING HUT
END RTE. 76

76

29

76 (ALTERNATE)

(76-H)

R I V E R

Elk Mountain Lodge

CASTLE CREEK RD.

(76-G)

(76-F)

Arthur Mtn

ASHCROFT SKI   W E S T
TOURING CENTER & PARKING
BEGIN RTES. 31, 32, 74 & 76 (ALTERNATE)

Toklat Lodge

Ashcroft

32

31

31

74

Waterfall

Gulch

Ashcroft Mtn

Campground

Difficult

Creek

GOODWIN GREEN
SKI TOURING HUT
END RTE. 75

29

END RTE. 29

Gold
Hill

31

PITKIN CO.

GUNNISON CO.

75

EXPRESS CREEK RD. (TAYLOR PASS RD.)

(76-E)

31

END RTE. 31
BEGIN RTE. 75

JOINS MAP
ON PG. 101

MARKLEY SKI
TOURING HUT
END RTE. 74

76 (ALTERNATE)

31

76 (ALTERNATE)

31

31

(31-A)

N

Taylor
Pass

0   ¼   ½ mi.
0   ½   1 km.

Ashcroft Mountain, left, and the Express Creek drainage, right. The obvious avalanche chutes run over the Express Creek Road. (Lou Dawson photo)

ski up Express Creek. To park at Ashcroft obey the signs. If in doubt, ask for information at the office.

To begin the tour, follow a public access route that leaves from the parking area near the Ashcroft Ghost Town and leads across the valley to the Express Creek Road (Taylor Pass Road), on the east side of the valley. If in doubt about this portion of the route, inquire at the Ski Touring Center office near the parking area.

Once you're on the east side of the valley, ski up the Express Creek Road as it makes a long climbing traverse to the south. In about a mile the road will cross the lower portion of an avalanche path that comes down the west side of Ashcroft Mountain, and less than ½ mile past this slope the road takes you across another. The traditional—and still best way—to deal with these slopes is simply to cross them with all the necessary precautions. They are relatively inactive, and slide only two or three times a year. If conditions are extremely dangerous it is possible—though difficult—to avoid these slopes by dropping lower into the Express Creek drainage. This alternative is not recommended because of the difficult bushwhacking and route finding it entails. You're probably better off, if avalanche conditions are deemed too risky, to turn back at the first avalanche slope and head home.

After you cross the slopes mentioned above, you'll pass through some sparse aspen forests, and about two miles from Ashcroft you'll come to a faint trail that forks to the right (leaving the main road cut). This is the trail to the Markley Hut (Route 74); there may be a sign at the fork that says Touring Hut. Take the trail to the hut, then ski up the valley past the hut, staying in the middle part of the valley to avoid avalanche slopes on both sides. Ski to the head of the valley where the map shows the road coming back near the creek. Get back on the road here and follow it to the hairpin turn that would head you up a long, dangerous switchback to Taylor Pass. Stay away from the switchback route by leaving the road at the hairpin and continuing north up the drainage. You can follow the last portion of the Express Creek drainage directly north to the Richmond Hill-McArthur Mountain area of Route 29. From here ski a short way east to Gold Hill.

A shorter way to the Gold Hill area is to head northeast up Express Creek past the hairpin a short way, then climb in an easterly direction to the nearby saddle on the county line (31-A). From here follow a high traverse northerly to Gold Hill.

Avalanche notes: Be aware of the large slide paths on the southwest side of Ashcroft Mountain.

32 Pearl Pass from Ashcroft

Difficulty: Advanced
Time: 8 hours to Pearl Pass
Distance: 8 miles
Elevation gain: 3,200 feet
Starting elevation: 9,498 feet
USGS 7.5 minute maps: Hayden Peak, Pearl Pass

Map—page 101

This route serves several ski touring huts (see Routes 72, 73, and 77) and connects to Crested Butte (Route 71). It is also a scenic tour in its own right.

Drive the Castle Creek Road to Ashcroft (see Routes 24 and 31).

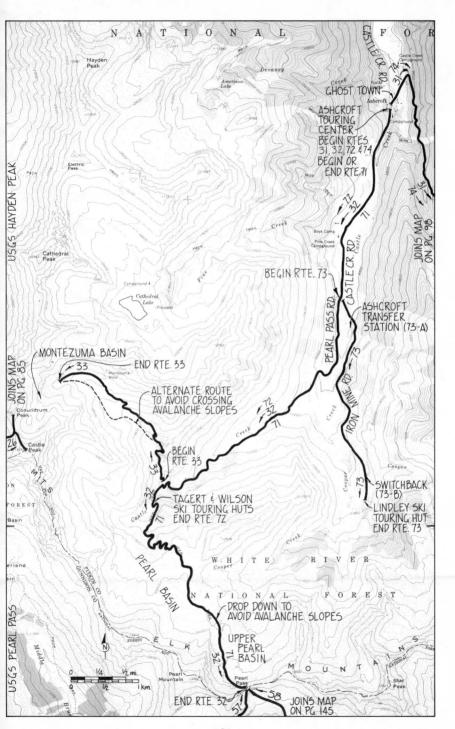

N A T I O N A L   F O R

Hayden
Peak

Devaney

American
Lake

CASTLE CR. RD.

Castle Creek
Campground

74

31

GHOST TOWN

Ashcroft

ASHCROFT
TOURING
CENTER
BEGIN RTES.
31, 32, 72 &74
BEGIN OR
END RTE. 71

Campground

Mine

31

74

Electric
Pass

TRAIL

PACK

72
32

Boys Camp

71

JOINS MAP
ON PG. 98

Creek

Pine Creek
Campground

Cathedral
Peak

PACK

Creek

TRAIL

Pine

Campground

Cathedral
Lake - Prospect

BEGIN RTE. 73

PEARL PASS RD.

CASTLE CR. RD.

Castle

ASHCROFT
TRANSFER
STATION (73-A)

USGS HAYDEN PEAK

MONTEZUMA BASIN

33

END RTE. 33

Montezuma
Mine

ALTERNATE ROUTE
TO AVOID CROSSING
AVALANCHE SLOPES

IRON MINE RD.

73

JOINS MAP ON PG. 85

Conundrum
Peak

MTS

26

Castle
Peak

BEGIN
RTE. 33

33

72
32
71

Creek

Creek

73

73

Cooper

SWITCHBACK
(73-B)

LINDLEY SKI
TOURING HUT
END RTE. 73

Basin

F O R E S T

32

Castle

TAGERT & WILSON
SKI TOURING HUTS
END RTE. 72

Cooper

erland

PEARL BASIN

W. H I T E   R I V E R

Creek

Cooper

PITKIN CO.
GUNNISON CO.

USGS PEARL PASS

Middle

N A T I O N A L   F O R E S T

DROP DOWN TO
AVOID AVALANCHE SLOPES

M O U N T A I N S

N A T I O N A L   F O R

N

FOREST

ELK

RD.

UPPER
PEARL
BASIN

32

71

Pearl
Mountain

Star
Peak

0   1/4   1/2 MI.

1/2   1 km.

END RTE. 32

Pearl
Pass

51

58

51

JOINS MAP
ON PG. 145

101

In upper Pearl Basin. Pearl Pass is the low point on the ridge. (Lou Dawson photo)

From Ashcroft, ski up the snow-covered Castle Creek Road for about two miles to its intersection with the Pearl Pass Road on the right. This intersection may be marked by a temporary sign that designates the directions of the Tagert and Lindley huts (Routes 72, 73). Just past the intersection there is a sign on the Pearl Pass Road that says "Narrow Rough Road 4-Wheel Drive Only." Follow the Pearl Pass Road as it passes under some avalanche chutes on the right, then begins the climb up to Pearl Basin and Pearl Pass. The route up to timberline stays on the road and is easy to follow because of the cut through the trees. It is common for the trail to be packed all the way to the huts just below timberline. After timberline, the route to Pearl Pass requires careful map reading. Take care to ski far enough to the southeast in Pearl Basin so as not to ski over one of the tempting passes on the ridge before the real Pearl Pass. For the return follow the same route, taking care not to drop down into Cooper Creek.

Avalanche notes: The worst section of the route is the slope just below the pass. At times it is wind loaded and dangerous; other times it is wind scoured and safe. Pearl Basin is fairly safe, since it is mostly low angled, although there can be pockets of unstable snow here and there on small headwalls. Pay attention to the large avalanche paths threatening the trail before it climbs out of the Castle Creek Valley. If conditions are questionable, skirt these areas by skiing farther out toward the center of the valley. If you do this, be careful not to ski past the point where you can regain the Pearl Pass Road.

33 Spring and Summer Skiing on Montezuma Glacier

Difficulty: Intermediate
Time: Depends on route
Distance: ¾ to 3 miles, depending on season
Elevation gain: Approximately 1,000 feet, depending on season
Starting elevation: Ashcroft, 9,498 feet
USGS 7.5 minute map: Hayden Peak

Map—page 101

Though this is not really a glacier, it is one of the largest permanent snowfields in Colorado. A beautiful place, it is set above timberline under the north face of 14,265-foot Castle Peak (see Route 26). Spring and summer skiing have been popular here for years.

Most people ski the lower portion of the snowfield below the small upper basin underneath Castle's north face. The upper basin itself is excellent, and with the right conditions it is possible to ski off the summit of Castle, down the beautiful gully to the northeast of the summit, then down the basin and the rest of the snowfield— a great ski descent.

Drive the Castle Creek Road to Ashcroft (see Routes 24 and 31). To reach Montezuma Basin, ski, hike, or drive (depending on the season) from Ashcroft and up the Pearl Pass Road (see Route 32). After the steep switchbacks about four miles out of Ashcroft, the Montezuma Road leaves the Pearl Pass Road and heads up to the right into a hanging valley. The road follows the right side of the valley to its terminus at the snowfield. These roads require four-wheel drive.

Avalanche notes: This area should be skied only in the spring and summer, when the snow is well consolidated.

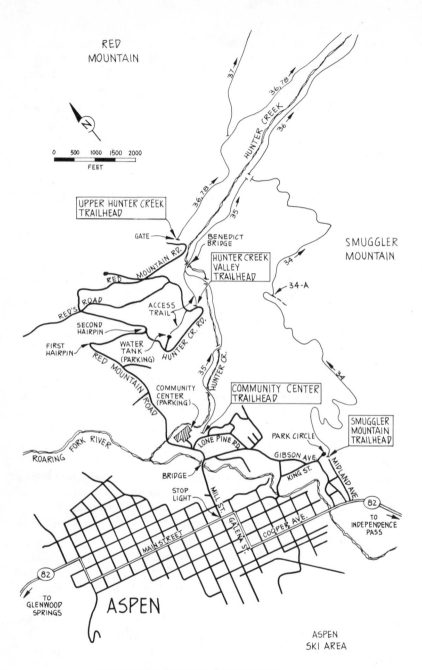

RED
MOUNTAIN

N

0   500 1000 1500 2000
FEET

UPPER HUNTER CREEK
TRAILHEAD

GATE

BENEDICT
BRIDGE

HUNTER CREEK
VALLEY
TRAILHEAD

SMUGGLER
MOUNTAIN

RED MOUNTAIN RD.

RED'S ROAD

ACCESS
TRAIL

34

34-A

SECOND
HAIRPIN

FIRST
HAIRPIN

WATER
TANK
(PARKING)

HUNTER CR. RD.

RED MOUNTAIN ROAD

HUNTER CR.

34

COMMUNITY
CENTER
(PARKING)

COMMUNITY CENTER
TRAILHEAD

ROARING FORK RIVER

LONE PINE RD.

PARK CIRCLE

SMUGGLER
MOUNTAIN
TRAILHEAD

GIBSON AVE.

BRIDGE

KING ST.

MIDLAND AVE.

STOP
LIGHT

MILL ST.

GALENA ST.

COOPER AVE.

82

TO
INDEPENDENCE
PASS

MAIN STREET

82

TO
GLENWOOD
SPRINGS

ASPEN

ASPEN
SKI AREA

HUNTER CREEK

DETAIL OF HUNTER CREEK TRAILHEADS.
FOR TOPOGRAPHICAL INFORMATION SEE
MAP ON PAGE 107.

34 Smuggler Mountain-Hunter Creek Access Trail

Difficulty: Novice
Time: 2 ½ hours
Distance: 3 miles to Hunter Creek
Elevation gain: 900 feet
Starting elevation: 7,900 feet
USGS 7.5 minute map: Aspen

Maps—pages 104 and 107

To the east of Aspen is the beautiful hanging valley of Hunter Creek. For many years this has been one of the area's most popular places for relaxed ski touring. The only problem with skiing in Hunter Creek is that access from Aspen is difficult. The area is separated from the town by a great deal of private land, and since it is a hanging valley the ski trails leading there from town are steep climbs of about 800 vertical feet. Remember that the parking areas and trailheads can change because of access problems.

This snow-covered road is probably the best way to ski in and out from the Hunter Creek Valley. To reach the start of this route, drive east out of Aspen on Highway 82 (toward Independence Pass). While still within the city limits, take a left on Midland Avenue just after crossing a bridge over the Roaring Fork River. Drive north on Midland into the Midland Park Condominium Development, then park. Just past the last building on the east edge of the development, the snow-covered Smuggler Mountain Road climbs up and left—there is a sign here for alternative vehicle access. When the Centennial Housing Project is complete, the official Smuggler Mountain Road will leave from Park Circle instead of Midland Park. There will be parking near Park Circle. Ski along the road as it switchbacks up the mountain. In about a mile you will arrive at a flat area where the road forks. Follow the left fork (34-A), which contours for a short way then drops about 400 vertical feet into Hunter Creek. Return the same way, or via the Community Center Trail (see Route 35), or ski to the Upper Hunter Creek trailhead (see Route 36).

Avalanche notes: There is usually no danger on this route. At rare times there could be problems with some of the open areas on the side of Smuggler Mountain.

35   Community Center-Hunter Creek Access Trail

Difficulty: Intermediate
Time: 1 ½ hours to Hunter Creek
Distance: 1 mile
Elevation gain: 800 feet
Starting elevation: 7,900 feet
USGS 7.5 minute map: Aspen

Maps—pages 104 and 107

This trail is very steep and more of a hassle than it is worth as a ski access route for the Hunter Creek Valley. But if you enjoy steep, narrow downhills, it is an exciting way to leave the valley.

To find the downhill end of this trail, drive Mill Street north from the stoplight next to the Jerome Hotel in central Aspen. Drive down the Mill Street hill and over a bridge that crosses the Roaring Fork River. Just beyond the bridge, you will see a sign for the Community Center. Take a hard right into the Community Center, and park in the designated area. Follow the signs to the trail. To avoid confusion, remember that the actual trail begins next to the Hunter Creek Properties 100 building and is marked with a detailed sign.

To find the uphill end of this trail, simply ski down the south side of Hunter Creek. The trail is obvious.

Avalanche notes: This is a safe route.

36   Hunter Creek Valley

Difficulty: Novice
Time: An easy day
Distance: 7 mile loop trip plus your access route
Elevation gain: 700 feet, within the valley
Starting elevation: Depends on access route
USGS 7.5 minute maps: Aspen, Thimble Rock

Maps—pages 104 and 107

Routes on both sides of the valley are excellent for intermediate skiers. These trails are easy to follow all the way to Thimble Rock, where the skiing and route finding become difficult. A good way to

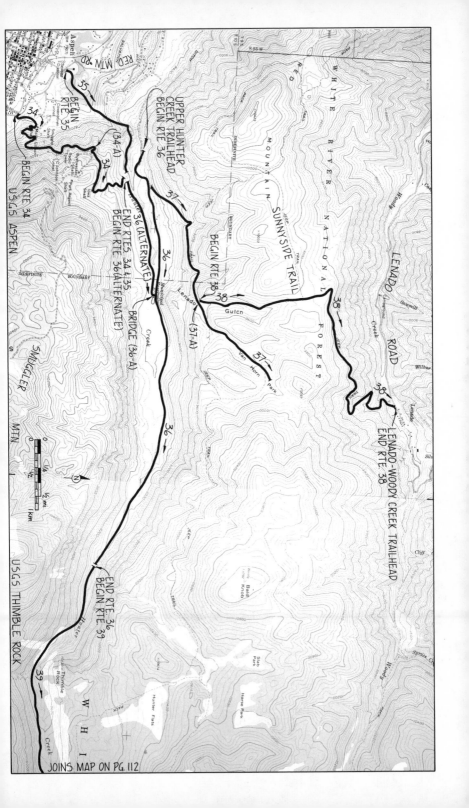

Aspen
New York
Tunnel
Midland
RED MTN RD.
35
BEGIN RTE 35
34
(34-A)
34
BEGIN RTE 34
USGS ASPEN
INDEFINITE BOUNDARY
SMUGGLER MTN
USGS THIMBLE ROCK

UPPER HUNTER CREEK TRAILHEAD BEGIN RTE 36
37
36
END RTES 34 & 35 BEGIN RTE 36 (ALTERNATE)
RTE 36 (ALTERNATE)
BRIDGE (36-A)
Creek
36
36
END RTE 36 BEGIN RTE 39
39
Thimble Rock
Hunter
Creek

WHITE RIVER NATIONAL FOREST
MOUNTAIN SUNNYSIDE TRAIL
BOUNDARY
BEGIN RTE 38
38
38
Lenado
Gulch
(37-A)
37
Van Horn Park
Bald Knob
Slab Park
Horse Park
W H I
JOINS MAP ON PG. 112

LENADO ROAD
Campground
Sawmill
Lenado
Wilber
38
38
LENADO-WOODY CREEK TRAILHEAD END RTE 38
Cliff
Spruce Cr.
Woody Cr.

0   ¼   ½   1 mi.
0   ¼   ½   1 Km.
(N)

enjoy Hunter Creek is to ski a loop using the reservoir bridge (36-A) at the upper end of the valley.

The valley may be gained in one of four ways. Two of these—the Smuggler Mountain-Hunter Creek Access Trail (Route 34) and the Community Center-Hunter Creek Access Trail (Route 35)—are described on the preceding pages. The other two accesses begin on Red Mountain and entail the least amount of elevation gain. To reach them, follow Mill Street in Aspen north ½ mile to the bridge crossing the Roaring Fork River (see Route 34). After crossing the bridge, take a left curve and stay on the main road; this is the Red Mountain Road. Follow it for a mile to just before the second hairpin turn, about halfway up through the residential section. Here you leave the main road and turn to the right on a spur. There may be a sign at this turn that says Hunter Creek Trail Parking and points to the right with an arrow. Follow the spur road and watch for a water tank on the left after a short way. Head up the

Gate at the Upper Hunter Creek trailhead on Red Mountain. (Lou Dawson photo)

driveway that leads behind the tank to a parking turnaround—
park here. This is the highest public parking on Red Mountain.
From here you have two choices: (1) you can follow the well-signed
trail that leads into Hunter Creek Valley by joining a spur of the
Hunter Creek Trail just behind the water tank (see Route 35), or (2)
you can continue up the Hunter Creek Road and follow it uphill to
the Upper Hunter Creek Trailhead, where it rejoins the Red
Mountain Road.

The Upper Hunter Creek trailhead is the closest to Hunter Creek
Valley, but there is no parking. So have a friend drop you off. You
can then arrange to be picked up at any one of the access
trailheads (see Routes 34 and 35). To reach the Upper Hunter Creek
Trailhead, follow the Red Mountain Road to the turnoff to the
Hunter Creek Trail Parking Area. Stay on the Red Mountain Road
and follow it uphill to a large flat area where the well-signed Red's
Road heads left and right. Do not turn onto Red's Road; just
continue north toward the top of Red Mountain. The road climbs
up and to the right around a switchback. Just before the last house
on the road, there is a gate on the right with a sign welcoming
hikers and horses. The dirt road past this gate is the highest access
to Hunter Creek and leads to a well-defined trail cut through brush
and aspen trees on the north side of the valley.

Avalanche notes: There is minimal avalanche danger. Be
aware of the occasional steep open slopes on the sides of the valley.

37   Hunter Creek to Van Horn Park

Difficulty: Novice
Time: 6 hours round trip
Distance: 6 miles round trip from Hunter Creek
Elevation gain: 1,000 feet
Starting elevation: Depends on access route
USGS 7.5 minute map: Aspen

Map—page 107

For the up and coming off-piste downhiller, Van Horn Park
provides some gentle practice terrain. Climb up to the park by
finding the upper jeep road on the north side of the Hunter Creek
Valley (see Route 36). A simple way to do this is to locate the barbed
wire fence that heads up the hill north from the big white teepee at
the lower end of the valley. The road begins on the uphill side of the
fence near a green steel gate a few hundred yards from the teepee.

Entering Van Horn Park from the west. Van Horn Saddle is obvious at the upper end of the park. (Lou Dawson photo)

Follow this road as it climbs northeast for about 1 ¾ miles to a large flat open area (37-A). Just before this open area, the Lenado Trail (see Route 38) splits off to the north. Ski across this area, then head up a gulch to the left (north), after which you will soon break out of the trees into Van Horn Park. Because the roads in this area are numerous and for the most part unsigned, be sure to read your map carefully.

Avalanche notes: The trail up to the park leads through heavily wooded terrain that is safe from avalanches. Some of the slopes on the park could slide during the worst possible conditions, but to the author's knowledge they never have. Take reasonable precautions.

38   Hunter Creek to or from Lenado

Difficulty: Intermediate
Time: 6 hours one way
Distance: 6 miles
Elevation gain: 1,200 feet
Starting elevation: 8,600 feet
USGS 7.5 minute map: Aspen

Map—page 107

This trip connects the Hunter Creek Valley with the small logging town of Lenado that lies in the next valley to the north. The problem with this tour is that most of the trail is in a dense forest with numerous false trails, and there are few landmarks for map reading. If you have not done this tour before, be sure to use map and compass along with these directions. A trail may be broken—but be sure it is the correct one!

Follow Route 37 to the large flat open area that you gain by the jeep road. Just before breaking out of the aspen trees into this area, take a hard left onto the Lenado Gulch Trail. This trail follows a wide cut through heavy timber in a northerly direction (as marked on the USGS *Aspen* map). The crucial intersections are unsigned. Be careful not to get on the Sunnyside Trail that climbs up Red Mountain. If you are on the correct trail you will soon arrive at the steep hillside that drops into the Woody Creek drainage and Lenado. Be sure to find the trail here; it is an old mule track cut into the side of the hill that drops to the east in a long traverse. The mule trail avoids all the impassable timber—do not attempt to ski directly down into the valley. Arrange a pickup in Lenado or ski back to Aspen.

To begin the trip from Lenado, drive to Lenado by taking the Woody Creek Road that turns off Highway 82, six miles west of Aspen. Drive the Woody Creek Road just over two miles to an unsigned hard right. Turn here onto the Lenado Road (this turn is just past the Woody Creek Trailer Park). Follow the Lenado Road eight miles to Lenado.

Find the trail by driving through the center of town (a small group of buildings on both sides of the road) and parking near the large open space on the right. Park well off the road. At the upper end of the open area, ski up a snow covered road through the trees in an easterly direction. After a few hundred feet of skiing, the road will fork. The left fork is the start of the mule trail mentioned

111

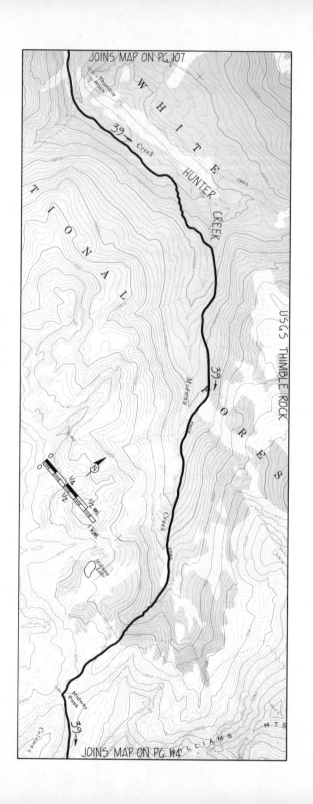

WHITE

Thimble
Rock

39

Creek

HUNTER

CREEK

TIONAL

USGS THIMBLE ROCK

TRAIL

39

Mammoth

FOREST

Creek

TRAIL

0

0   ½ mi

¼

½   1 Km

Midway
Pass

Cal. State R.

WILLIAMS

MTS

39

View of Midway Pass from Bald Knob. Some of the difficult route finding is in the forest at the lower left. (Lou Dawson photo)

above. The trail is obscure, making it tempting to ski to the west on the right fork of the road—but this fork dead-ends in about a mile.

Avalanche notes: This is a safe route.

39   Hunter Creek over Midway Pass to Independence Pass Road

Difficulty: Advanced
Time: Several days
Distance: 25 miles from Hunter Creek to the Independence Pass
    winter road closure
Elevation gain: 3,000 feet
Starting elevation: Depends on access route
USGS 7.5 minute maps: Aspen, Thimble Rock, New York Peak

Maps—pages 107, 112, and 114

Ski Route 36 (Hunter Creek) to Thimble Rock, where the valley closes off and there is no obvious trail. Continue up the valley here by crossing the creek several times to find a route through the brush and deadfall. If the creek is frozen hard, use it as a ski route. At the point where Midway Creek intersects Hunter Creek, find the trail cut through the trees on the left side of Midway Creek (as marked on the USGS *Thimble Rock* map). Follow the trail to Midway Pass. From the pass, if avalanche conditions are reasonable, take the trail marked on the USGS *Thimble Rock, Mount*

Champion, and *Independence Pass* maps that drops to the Independence Pass Road. Ski the Independence Road out to civilization (see Route 60).

Avalanche notes: If conditions preclude the traverse after the pass, it is possible to bushwhack through dense timber directly down Coleman Creek to Independence Road. The route is safe for the most part, but watch for questionable spots above timberline. Sound judgment and skilled route finding are essential for the safe completion of this route.

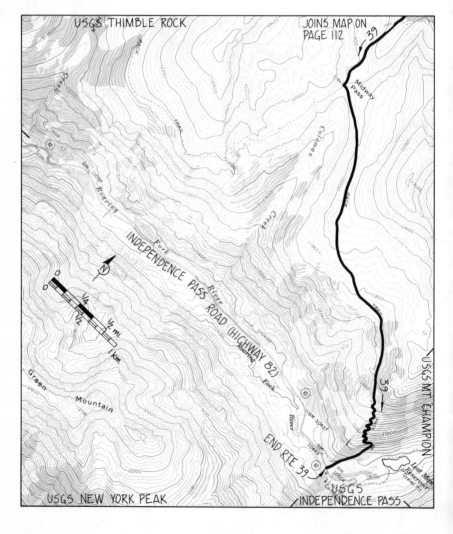

CHAPTER FIVE

Crested Butte Area

Much of Crested Butte's excellent ski touring is near the town, and several trips in this chapter begin within walking distance of any breakfast place. The town's high elevation—8,900 feet—and heavy snowfalls, make the skiing last from early winter to late spring.

Checking out a small cornice near the summit of Red Lady. (Gnurps photo)

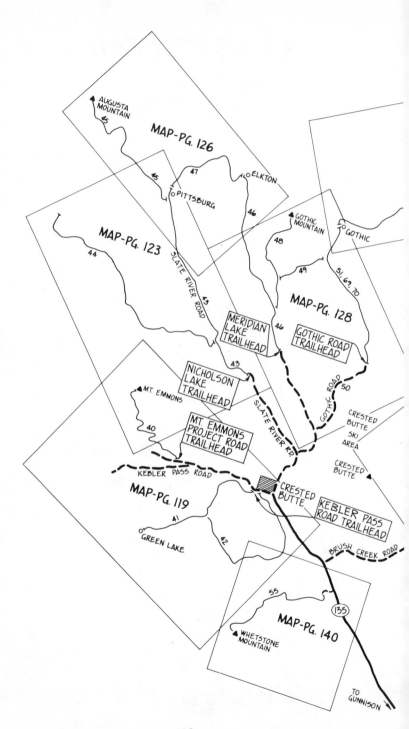

AUGUSTA MOUNTAIN
45

MAP-PG. 126

45 47 ELKTON
PITTSBURG 46

MAP-PG. 123

44

SLATE RIVER ROAD

43

GOTHIC MOUNTAIN

48

GOTHIC

51, 69, 70

49

MAP-PG. 128

MERIDIAN LAKE TRAILHEAD 46

GOTHIC ROAD TRAILHEAD

43

NICHOLSON LAKE TRAILHEAD

MT. EMMONS

SLATE RIVER RD.

GOTHIC ROAD

50

CRESTED BUTTE SKI AREA

MT. EMMONS PROJECT ROAD TRAILHEAD

40

CRESTED BUTTE

KEBLER PASS ROAD

MAP-PG. 119

CRESTED BUTTE

KEBLER PASS ROAD TRAILHEAD

41

GREEN LAKE

42

BRUSH CREEK ROAD

135

55

MAP-PG. 140

WHETSTONE MOUNTAIN

TO GUNNISON

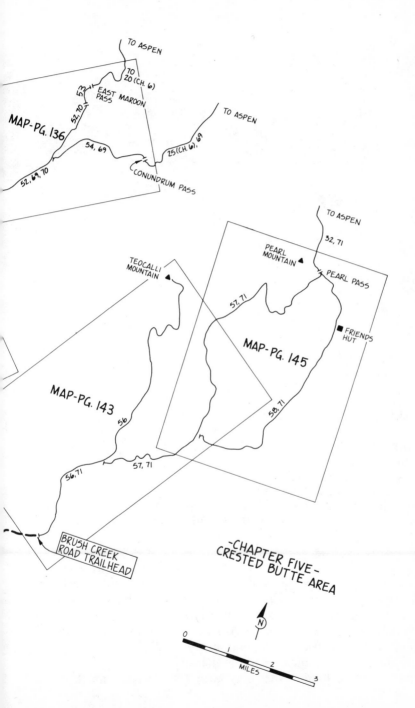

MAP-PG. 136

TO ASPEN

70
20 (CH. 6)

53
52,70

EAST MAROON
PASS

TO ASPEN

25 (CH. 6), 69

54, 69

52, 69, 70

CONUNDRUM PASS

TO ASPEN

32, 71

PEARL
MOUNTAIN ▲

PEARL PASS

TEOCALLI
MOUNTAIN ▲

57, 71

MAP-PG. 145

■ FRIENDS
HUT

MAP-PG. 143

56

58, 71

56, 71

57, 71

BRUSH CREEK
ROAD TRAILHEAD

-CHAPTER FIVE-
CRESTED BUTTE AREA

N

0   1   2   3
MILES

117

Climbing Red Lady. Whetstone Mountain, right, and Crested Butte, left, are visible in the distance. (Gnurps photo)

40   Red Lady Basin

Difficulty: Advanced
Time: 6 hours round trip
Distance: 4 miles round trip
Elevation gain: 2,500 feet
Starting elevation: 9,000 feet
USGS 7.5 minute maps: Oh-Be-Joyful, Mount Axtell

Map—page 119

Clearly dominating the views to the northwest of Crested Butte is the peak named Mount Emmons on the map, but called Red Lady by most locals. The mountain has been the subject of an environmental controversy because it lies over a valuable molybdenum deposit claimed by the AMAX Corporation. The company has some industrial operations on the south shoulder that are off-limits to skiers, but does not seem to object to people skiing from the summit as long as they stay away from the industrial sites.

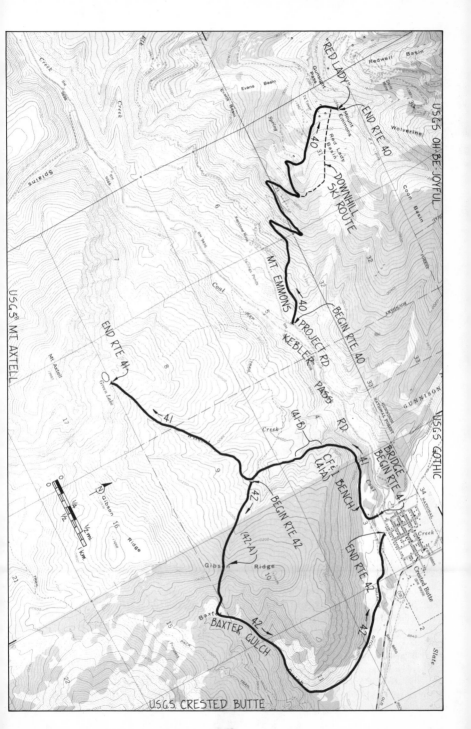

Best access to the summit is via the southeast ridge—the one to the left of the big bowl as you look up from the town of Crested Butte. To gain the ridge, drive up the Kebler Pass Road from the west end of Crested Butte and park at the fork about 1 ½ miles up the road where the Mount Emmons Project Road heads up to the right. There is a small sign here. Walk up the steep road a short way to the gully, where there may be a sign announcing the Skiers and Hikers Route.

This gully is the lower portion of the Red Lady Basin drainage. Even though the sign points directly into the gully, using the gut of the gully for a route is ill advised, since the steep open slopes on its sides create a great deal of avalanche hazard. To avoid this dangerous initial section, either scramble up the slopes to the left or take the sparsely timbered slopes to the right and cross the drainage higher up to gain the southeast ridge. The route on the ridge is obvious—it stays on the crest except for a few minor deviations to avoid dense timber and steep sections. For the descent, the best skiing is in the basin, but if conditions are dangerous in the basin the ascent route has some good skiing.

Avalanche notes: There are many good lines to ski in Red Lady Basin, and it has been skied many times without incident in the winter. Avalanche activity is usually in the form of direct-action slabs just after storms. Once every few winters the whole bowl cuts loose in one massive slide. A relatively safe route in the bowl can be skied by linking up several subtle ribs and the large, obvious shelves. The expert back-country skier will be able to ski this bowl safely during any season. The less experienced should wait for a safe spring morning to make the descent.

41   Gibson Ridge to Green Lake

Difficulty: Novice
Time: 3 hours
Distance: 3 ½ miles
Elevation gain: 1,800 feet to Green Lake
Starting elevation: 9,000 feet
USGS 7.5 minute maps: Mount Axtell, Crested Butte

Map—page 119

On the west end of Crested Butte, the Kebler Pass Road crosses a small bridge over Coal Creek, then climbs a steep hill. While still on

Skiing up Red Lady, with Kebler Pass area in the background. (Gnurps photo)

the town side of this bridge, ski south across a small field next to the Coal Creek Condominiums, then climb a short, steep hill south to the large flat area known as the CF&I Bench (41-A). The steep timbered hillside rising to the south is the north side of Gibson Ridge.

Ski the CF&I Bench to the west until an obvious road cut climbs up and a bit to the left. Once on this road you will be skiing a steep traverse in a westerly direction. After about ¾ mile on this traverse the trail will flatten out (41-B). From here you will see an obvious road cut through the trees to the south, wandering up to the top of Gibson Ridge (see Route 42).

To reach Green Lake, take this road cut for about ¼ mile, then take a more obscure trail that branches off to the southwest and leads into the Wildcat Creek drainage and up to Green Lake. Navigation is confusing on this route—be ready to use map and compass. Return via the same route or follow Gibson Ridge to Baxter Gulch (see Route 42).

Avalanche notes: This route is extremely safe. The Green Lake area is exposed to some large avalanches off Mount Axtell, so be observant about where you make your lunch stop.

42   Gibson Ridge to Baxter Gulch

Difficulty: Novice
Time: 6 hours
Distance: 7 miles
Elevation gain: 2,000 feet
Starting elevation: 9,000 feet
USGS 7.5 minute maps: Mount Axtell, Crested Butte

Map—page 119

This trip includes a bit of downhill skiing. Gain a saddle (42-A) on Gibson ridge (see Route 41). From here ski to the east down into Baxter Gulch, then on down into the main East River Valley. Return to Crested Butte by skiing a mile up the main valley.

Avalanche notes: Be careful of small sluffs in Baxter Gulch and the large paths that come down off the east end of Gibson Ridge.

43   Slate River Road

Difficulty: Novice
Time: 6 hours round trip
Distance: 4 ½ miles one way
Elevation gain: Minimal
Starting elevation: 9,000 feet
USGS 7.5 minute map: Oh-Be-Joyful

Map—page 123

The Slate River Road provides auto access for several tours. In winter, it is closed at Nicholson Lake. In early fall and late spring, you can drive up the road quite a way into the heart of the Elks.

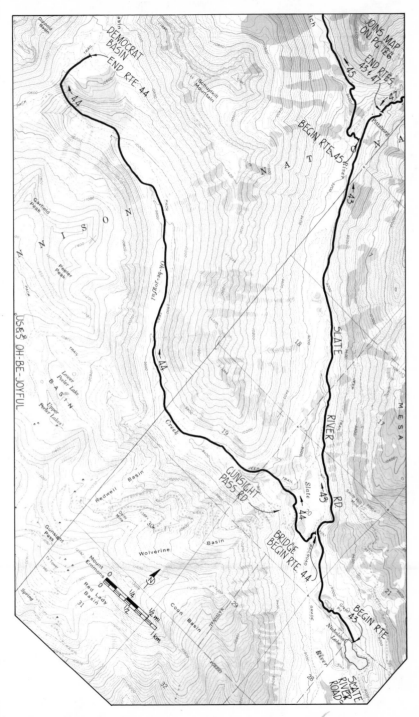

From the east end of the town of Crested Butte drive about ¾ of a mile up Mount Crested Butte (Gothic) Road. The Slate River Road takes off to the left at this point (there is a sign, but it may be covered by snow). Drive the Slate River Road about 2 ½ miles to Nicholson Lake. Here the road forks; the left leg heads up a hill to the Nicholson Lake subdivision; the right leg continues along the Slate River Road. In the winter the Slate River Road is closed at this fork. Park where the plow has widened the road. The snow-covered portion of the road follows the east side of the valley and makes a good ski trail all the way to the small group of summer homes called Pittsburg.

Avalanche notes: There is little danger for the first ½ mile or so. After that there are a few paths that cross the road when they run big. Plan your trip for a time of least hazard.

44   Oh-Be-Joyful Creek

Difficulty: Intermediate to advanced
Time: 7 hours round trip
Distance: 7 miles one way to Democrat Basin
Elevation gain: 1,600 feet
Starting elevation: 9,000 feet
USGS 7.5 minute map: Oh-Be-Joyful

Map—page 123

Ski the Slate River Road (see Route 43) from Nicholson Lake for about a mile. Down to the left you will see a bridge crossing the Slate River. Cross here, then follow the Gunsight Pass Road to the first switchback as marked on the USGS *Oh-Be-Joyful* map. Leave the road at this point and contour into the Oh-Be-Joyful drainage. The trail up the drainage is on the north side of the creek, as shown on the map.

The first several miles of the trail are good intermediate touring. The remainder of the trail to the Democrat Basin area is an excellent advanced trip. The ski to the Democrat Basin area makes a good overnight trip.

Avalanche notes: The first two miles of the trail are fairly safe, though they do pass below several paths that slide infrequently. Take normal precautions here (avoid picnicking in the runout zone). After the first two miles the trail is more exposed, though exposure may be reduced by crossing to the other side of the creek.

Skiing fresh powder. (Michael Kennedy photo)

45 Mount Augusta

Difficulty: Intermediate
Time: 6 hours round trip
Distance: 6 miles round trip from Pittsburg
Elevation gain: 3,000 feet
Starting elevation: Depends on road access
USGS 7.5 minute map: Oh-Be-Joyful

Map—page 126

This is one of the best intermediate ski descents near Crested Butte. But it is only safe from avalanches after the spring snow consolidation. It is usually skied in late spring after the Slate River Road is drivable to Pittsburg. This area has one of the Elk's deepest snow packs due to a convergence of storm tracks and a massive uplift.

Drive the Slate River Road to Pittsburg (see Route 43). From

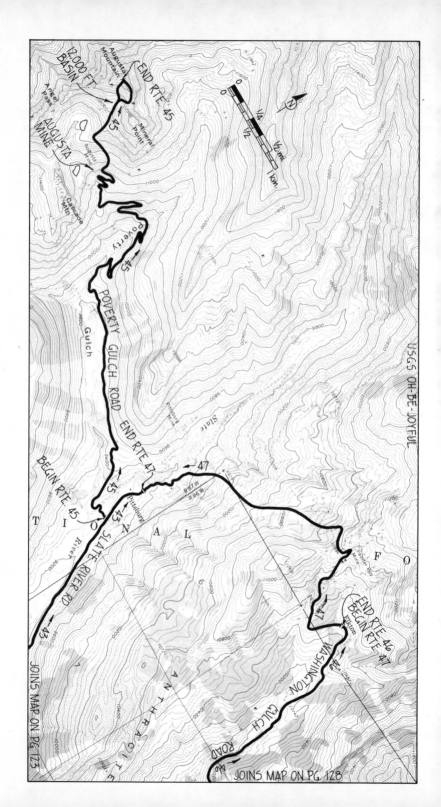

12,000 FT BASIN

Augusta Mountain

END RTE 45

Anna Peak

AUGUSTA MINE

Mineral Point

45

Augusta Mine

Cascade Mtn

POVERTY

45

POVERTY GULCH ROAD

Gulch

END RTE 47

BEGIN RTE 45

45

45

47

Pittsburg

R 87 W
R 86 W

Pitzsburg Mine

Slate

Pittsburg

TI O N A L

River

SLATE RIVER RD

11000

43

F O

Painter Boy Mine

END RTE 46
BEGIN RTE 47

Pixton

WASHINGTON

47

46

A N T H R A C I T E

WASHINGTON GULCH ROAD

46

47

46

JOINS MAP ON PG. 123

JOINS MAP ON PG. 128

U.S.G.S. OH-BE-JOYFUL

N

½ mi.

1 km.

there the route to the summit is simple: follow the Poverty Gulch Road (marked on the USGS *Oh-Be-Joyful* map) to the Augusta Mine. From the mine, head directly toward the summit; as you hike you will pass over the south flank of Mineral Point. Soon you will be in the 12,000-foot basin below Augusta's summit. From here you can clamber directly up the south face or ascend via the saddle between the summit and Mineral Point.

Although this is not a particularly high summit, the view to the west into Dark Canyon is superb. And the ski back down the south face is thoroughly enjoyable. Good variations for skiing can be made by dropping into the upper basin (the one with the lake). If you do ski in this direction, be sure to head back toward the road at the level of the mine. Cascade Mountain is too steep and rocky for good skiing.

Avalanche notes: Because this is a south-facing ski descent, spring skiers should be careful to make the requisite early start.

46   Washington Gulch to Elkton

Difficulty: Novice
Time: 7 hours round trip
Distance: 8 miles round trip
Elevation gain: 1,000 feet
Starting elevation: 9,600 feet
USGS 7.5 minute maps: Gothic, Oh-Be-Joyful

Maps—pages 126 and 128

This and the following three trips begin just past the Meridian Lake subdivision. To reach the subdivision, drive up the Mount Crested Butte (Gothic) Road from the east end of Crested Butte. Follow the road for 1 ¼ miles to the well-signed Washington Gulch-Meridian Lake Road that turns off to the left. Follow this road for about two miles to a snowplow turnaround just past the Meridian Lake subdivision. Parking is no problem.

This excellent tour continues along the snow-covered Washington Gulch Road to a small group of buildings called Elkton. Follow the Washington Gulch Road to the snowplow turnaround and parking area. From here stay to the right as you ski the snow-covered road leading up the valley (usually the road will have snowmobile or ski tracks). The road climbs a bit, then follows the right side of the valley to Elkton. The road is easy to follow in most places, though it can become obscured by wind-blown snow.

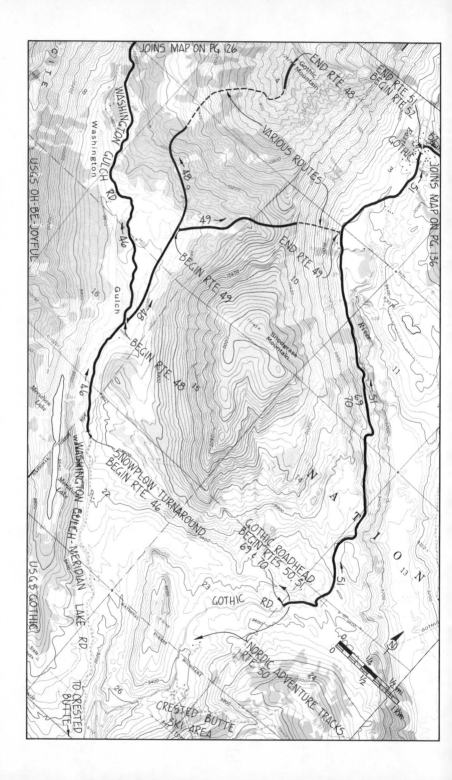

JOINS MAP ON PG. 126

END RTE 48

END RTE 51
BEGIN RTE 52

Gothic
Mountain

GOTHIC

WASHINGTON GULCH RD.

Washington

VARIOUS ROUTES

48
9

JOINS MAP ON PG. 136

USGS OH-BE-JOYFUL

OH-BE

Gulch

49

46

BEGIN RTE 49

END RTE 49

Snodgrass
Mountain

Meridian
Lake

48

BEGIN RTE 48

51

46

WASHINGTON GULCH-MERIDIAN LAKE RD.

N

A

T

I

O

N

SNOWPLOW TURNAROUND
BEGIN RTE. 46

GOTHIC ROADHEAD
BEGIN RTES 50, 51
69 & 70

USGS GOTHIC

GOTHIC RD.

51

GOTHIC

N

NORDIC ADVENTURE TRACKS
RTE 50

0   ¼

0   ¼   ½ mi.

½   1 km.

TO CRESTED BUTTE

CRESTED BUTTE
SKI AREA

Skiing up Washington Gulch toward Gothic Mountain. The ascent route follows the windblown ribs on the left. (Lou Dawson photo)

Read your map a bit and navigation will be no problem.

Avalanche notes: The first and last sections of the valley are safe, but the middle of the route can be threatened by some paths off Gothic Peak. Avoid traveling this route during times of extreme hazard.

47   Elkton to Pittsburg and out via Slate River

Difficulty: Advanced
Time: 8 hours
Distance: 12 miles for the whole trip, starting from the Meridian Lake roadhead
Elevation gain: 1,500 feet
Starting elevation: 9,400 feet
USGS 7.5 minute maps: Oh-Be-Joyful, Gothic

Map—page 126

This trip forms a long, enjoyable loop by connecting the Washington Gulch drainage with the Slate River drainage. Follow

Nature's art. (Michael Kennedy photo)

Route 46 to Elkton. From Elkton climb up the road that leads west to a low pass (this is the heavily mined area shown on the map). From the summit of the pass follow a snow-covered road cut as it drops gradually and traverses in a northerly direction. In ¼ mile or so you will have skied past several narrow gullies that drop down into the drainage below. Once past these gullies there is a great deal of excellent ski terrain. After skiing these nice open slopes, regain the road just before Pittsburg, then ski through Pittsburg and stay on the Slate River Road as it leads you to the Nicholson Lake roadhead (see Route 43).

Avalanche notes: There are a few paths crossing the Washington Gulch Road and the Slate River Road, but these run infrequently. There is danger of small pocket slabs on the route down from the pass. Take the usual precautions and be aware of prevailing conditions.

48   Gothic Mountain

Difficulty: Intermediate
Time: 7 hours round trip
Distance: 8 miles
Elevation gain: 3,000 feet
Starting elevation: 9,400 feet
USGS 7.5 minute maps: Gothic, Oh-Be-Joyful

Map—page 128

This is an excellent spring ski descent that should be on anyone's list. Take the Washington Gulch Road (see Route 46) for about two miles from the roadhead. From here simply climb a series of obvious and easily negotiated ribs up the south side of Gothic Mountain. The best ski routes follow any of the large gullies in the same area. Be aware of the gullies further to the north, as they end in cliffs.

Avalanche notes: Although this peak can be safely climbed in the winter by using the wind-scoured ribs on the west side, the gullies should only be skied in the spring after the snow has gone into the spring freeze-thaw cycle.

49   Washington Gulch to Gothic Road

Difficulty: Advanced
Time: 6 hours
Distance: 6 miles
Elevation gain: 1,000 feet
Starting elevation: 9,400 feet
USGS 7.5 minute maps: Gothic, Oh-Be-Joyful

Map—page 128

Follow the Washington Gulch Road (see Route 46). In about a mile, leave the road and climb up through trees and a few open areas to the obvious pass between Gothic Mountain and Snodgrass Mountain. From the pass, ski the beautiful slopes east and down to the Gothic Road (see Route 51). Follow the Gothic Road 3½ miles out to the Mount Crested Butte (Gothic) roadhead.

Avalanche notes: The route up the west side of the pass is fairly safe if you use the trees. The slopes down to the Gothic Road are prime avalanche terrain, and should be approached with care. There are some groves of trees and a few ribs on these slopes that can be linked into a semblance of a safe route.

50   Nordic Adventure Tracks

Difficulty: Novice
Time: Up to a full day
Distance: Varies with route
Elevation gain: Varies with route
Starting elevation: 9,400 feet
USGS 7.5 minute map: Gothic

Map—page 128

This is a series of well-maintained trails that wander about the ski resort area, up the Gothic Road (see Route 51), and around the south side of Snodgrass Mountain (to the west). They are maintained by the Nordic Adventure Program, a ski guide service operating under the auspices of the Crested Butte Mountain Resort. These trails should be skied with care since they are made with a track-setting machine and can be easily damaged by people walking, taking their dogs along, or skiing carelessly. A map showing the ski trails can be obtained at the resort's ticket office.

Drive up the Mount Crested Butte Ski Area (Gothic) Road from the east end of the town of Crested Butte. Drive on past the ski area, stay on the main road, and you will soon come to the road terminus ½ mile past the Mount Crested Butte city hall and fire station. This is the winter Gothic roadhead. In early fall or late spring the road may be open farther up the valley, either to the Crested Butte Stables or to the small town of Gothic.

From the Gothic roadhead, ski up the snow-covered Gothic Road for about ½ mile to the Crested Butte Stables. There is an obvious sign here announcing the beginning of the Nordic Adventure Tracks.

Avalanche notes: These trails lie mostly within the avalanche-controlled ski area. Skiers should remember that it is possible to ski out of this area into dangerous avalanche terrain.

Striding out on the nordic tracks at Crested Butte. (Gnurps photo)

51 Gothic Road to Gothic

Difficulty: Intermediate
Time: 5 hours round trip
Distance: 7 miles round trip
Elevation gain: 200 feet (on the return)
Starting elevation: 9,400 feet
USGS 7.5 minute map: Gothic

Map—page 128

From the Gothic roadhead (see Route 50), ski north on the snow-covered Gothic Road, as shown on the USGS *Gothic* map. After 3½ miles of gentle terrain, you will arrive at the small deserted

For all the work, there is a reward. (Michael Kennedy photo)

town of Gothic. This is a beautiful day tour and is usually facilitated by caretakers skiing to and from Gothic, who pack the trail. In its heyday Gothic was a booming mine town. Now it is the home of the Rocky Mountain Biological Laboratory, an outfit that does a great deal of important research into the surrounding ecology. The laboratory suspends most of its operations in the winter.

Avalanche notes: There are several paths on the northeast side of Snodgrass Mountain that occasionally run over the road trail. These are dangerous only during the most unstable times. Take normal precautions.

52   Gothic to Copper Lake

Difficulty: Intermediate
Time: 2 full days for the round trip in midwinter
Distance: 16 miles round trip from the Gothic roadhead
Elevation gain: 2,100 feet
Starting elevation: 9,500 feet
USGS 7.5 minute maps: Maroon Bells, Gothic

Map—page 136

The trip from Gothic to Copper Lake is reasonably safe, but strenuous because the trail is rarely broken past Judd Falls. Follow Route 51 to Gothic. From Gothic the route follows the road trail marked on the USGS *Maroon Bells* and *Gothic* maps. This road begins as a sharp right turn at the north end of Gothic, just past the last cabin on the right as you ski north from the center of town. Ski the road trail up the Copper drainage to the last stream crossing about three miles up. After this point the trail climbs some steep terrain to Copper Lake, and is difficult to find. Be prepared to use map, compass, and skilled route finding. If you venture too far to the west there is an impassable ravine, and too far to the east there is dense timber. Climbing skins are helpful. Return via the same route, or ski Routes 53 or 54.

Avalanche notes: There are several major but infrequent avalanches that run across the trail. The route crosses no fracture zones and is unsafe only during the most unstable times.

53   Copper Lake to East Maroon Pass

Difficulty: Advanced
Time: 1 hour
Distance: ½ mile
Elevation gain: 600 feet
Starting elevation: 11,200 feet
USGS 7.5 minute map: Maroon Bells

Map—page 136

This connecting route allows one to enjoy a nice ski up and back from East Maroon Pass to Copper Lake, and also forms part of the East Maroon Pass Route between Aspen and Crested Butte (see Route 70).

Follow Route 52 to Copper Lake. To reach the summit of East

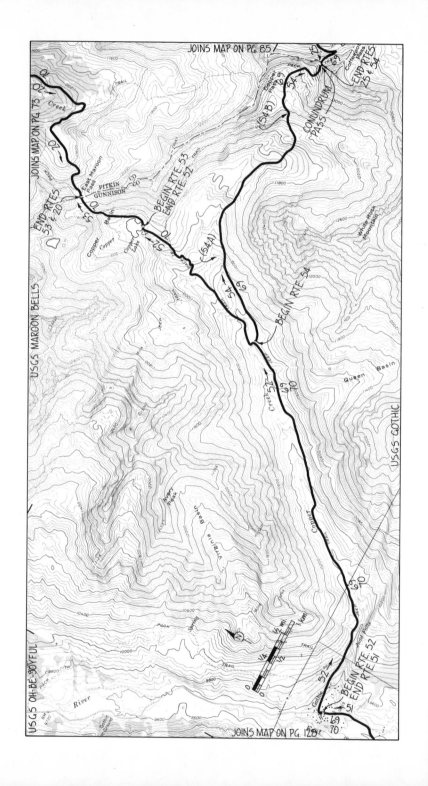

JOINS MAP ON PG. 73

USGS MAROON BELLS

USGS OH-BE-JOYFUL

USGS GOTHIC

END RTE. 53 & 20

PITKIN CO
GUNNISON CO

East Maroon Pass

Copper
Copper
Copper Lake

BEGIN RTE. 53
END RTE. 52

END RTES.
25 & 54

CONUNDRUM PASS

Conundrum Pass

BEGIN RTE. 54

Queen Basin

White Rock Mountain

Avery Peak

Virginia Basin

Copper Creek

BEGIN RTE. 52
END RTE. 51

Gothic

River

Creek

TRAIL

TRAIL

½ mi.
1 km
¼ ½
0

PACK

½ mi. 1 km

Climbing out of Gothic toward Copper Lake. (Lou Dawson photo)

Maroon Pass from Copper Lake, simply climb up the obvious face to the north of the lake. Return via the same route. Or ski Route 20 to the T Lazy 7 Guest Ranch roadhead and Aspen.

   Avalanche notes: The face above the lake is avalanche prone when snow covered. It can be negotiated without risk only after it has avalanched or been blown clear of snow. Luckily the wind hammers this exposure, and it is common for the slope to be safe.

Reaching the top of Conundrum Pass from the Crested Butte side. The wind-scoured snow is common. (Lou Dawson photo)

54   Conundrum Pass from Crested Butte

Difficulty: Advanced
Time: 10 hours
Distance: 10 miles
Elevation gain: 3,500 feet
Starting elevation: 9,500 feet
USGS 7.5 minute map: Gothic

Map—page 136

Follow Route 51 to Gothic. From there, follow the road trail (as marked on the USGS. *Gothic* map) up Copper Creek to the point below White Rock Mountain where the road trail makes a stream crossing, then turns north to Copper Lake (Route 52). Just before this stream crossing, leave the snow-covered road and head up the drainage toward Conundrum Pass (marked as Triangle Pass on the 1961 USGS map). Stay out of the actual streambed (54-A) (it becomes a small gorge) and hug the base of White Rock Mountain until it is time to make an obvious cut across the valley and toward the pass. Be careful that the pass you have chosen is really Conundrum Pass; it is easy to get confused and head for the pass at the head of the drainage.

The cut across the valley from the base of White Rock Mountain begins at timberline and leads directly to the small headwall below the hanging basin beneath Conundrum Pass (54-B). This small headwall is the most avalanche-prone portion of the route, but by careful route finding it can be safely negotiated during reasonably safe conditions. The hanging basin above the headwall is a good route the remainder of the way to the pass. From the top, there is a distinctive view of the mountains west of Crested Butte. Return via the same route or continue to Aspen via Routes 24 and 25 (and see Chapter 7).

Avalanche notes: There are several areas that should be treated with caution. The northwest slopes of White Rock Mountain should be skirted carefully, as should the headwall up to the hanging basin mentioned above. All these slopes slide infrequently, and will be no problem if treated with caution during times of less risk.

55 Main Summit of Whetstone Mountain from Highway 135

Difficulty: Intermediate to extreme
Time: 6 hours round trip
Distance: 2 miles one way
Elevation gain: 3,700 feet
Starting elevation: 8,800 feet
USGS 7.5 minute map: Crested Butte

Map—page 140

The impressive bulk of Whetstone Mountain rises to the south of the town of Crested Butte. The innumerable bowls and gullies that drop from the mountain's four summits provide a wealth of terrain

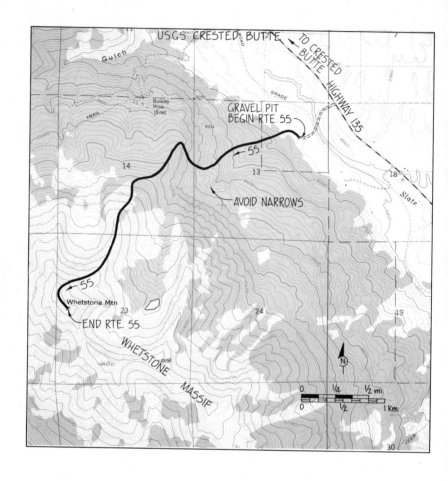

for spring skiing. If a mountain in the Crested Butte area had been designed for skiing, this would be it.

To climb Whetstone Mountain, drive about two miles southeast on Highway 135 (the main valley highway) from the town of Crested Butte. Across the valley to the southwest you will see the Mountain View Gravel Pit nestled beneath the northeast slopes of Whetstone Mountain. Take the gravel pit road across the river and park near the pit. Be sure to ask permission for parking. From here, ski back up the valley a short distance, then climb the big ridge forming the northwest side of the bowl east of the summit (on the USGS map, this is the bowl with the small lake). This ridge is a

Whetstone Mountain as seen from the north. The main summit is on the right, and Baxter Gulch is the drainage on the right. (Lou Dawson photo)

good route all the way to the summit. The standard descent follows the bowl to the point where it necks down, then traverses out onto the ascent ridge to avoid the narrows. Ski the open areas and glades on the ridge and drop back into the drainage below the narrows. There are many other descent routes off Whetstone. Take your pick and have fun exploring.

Avalanche notes: For complete safety, this peak should be skied early in the morning in spring, when the snow is frozen. It can also be skied during stable times in the winter.

56   Teocalli Summit from West Brush Creek

Difficulty: Advanced
Time: A long day or overnight
Distance: 7 miles to the summit from the ranch near the road terminus
Elevation gain: 4,000 feet
Starting elevation: 9,000 feet
USGS 7.5 minute maps: Gothic, Pearl Pass, Crested Butte

Map—page 143

This is an excellent winter climb because it features a ridge route with less avalanche danger than many other peaks of comparable altitude.

Drive down the valley out of Crested Butte for about two miles on Highway 135. Here you will see the Brush Creek Road turning off to the left. There are two signs marking the turn: one for the airport and one for Skyland Ranch. Turn onto the Brush Creek Road and drive to its terminus, probably a snowplow turnaround at the ranch about three miles up the road. Be careful to park out of the rancher's way, and control your dog if you have one along.

From the Brush Creek Road terminus, ski up the snow-covered Brush Creek Road for about 1 ¼ miles past the ranch. Take a right fork here into Brush Creek Valley. After you make the turn you will ski past several small cabins. Stay on the road trail marked on the USGS *Gothic* map for about a mile to the next intersection. Here the West Brush Creek Road climbs up a hill to the left and the main Brush Creek Road continues straight ahead. There may be a sign at this intersection. Follow West Brush Creek Road as it climbs over the hill, then contours into the West Brush Creek drainage.

Once in the West Brush Creek Valley (56-A), follow the creek for about a mile, then climb up the sparsely timbered slopes to the right that lead up to the saddle at timberline on Teocalli Ridge. From the saddle, follow the prominent south-facing ridge to the summit. The descent follows the same route—or, in spring, you can ski the beautiful "S" Gully west of the south ridge.

Avalanche notes: Avoid the open avalanche paths on the west side of Teocalli Ridge by staying in trees as much as possible during the ascent. The upper portion of the ridge (above timberline) is fairly narrow and wind blasted, making it relatively safe in the

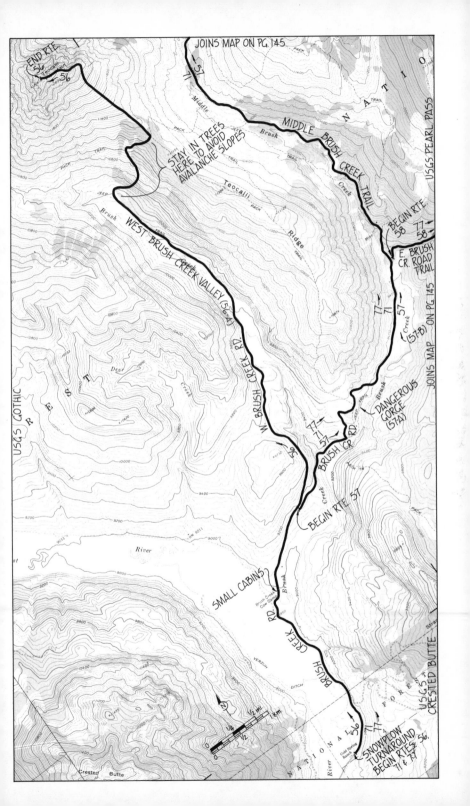

JOINS MAP ON PG. 145

winter. There is a section of the ridge lower down (just above timberline) that is wider and tends to collect a heavy snowload at times, but it is usually stabilized by wind compaction.

57   Middle Brush Creek to Pearl Pass

Difficulty: Advanced
Time: Probably overnight
Distance: 11 miles from the road terminus to the pass summit
Elevation gain: 3,800 feet
Starting elevation: 9,000 feet
USGS 7.5 minute maps: Gothic, Pearl Pass

Maps—pages 143 and 145

Take Route 56 to the intersection of West Brush Creek Road with main Brush Creek Road. Instead of taking the West Brush Creek fork, continue up main Brush Creek following the road trail on the map. In ½ mile you will come to an obvious narrowing in the valley (57-A). Here the trail climbs up through trees on the left side of the valley to avoid a small but dangerous gorge. After avoiding the gorge, the trail drops back to the creek and follows it for about a mile through a relatively flat area (57-B). Just after the confluence of Middle Brush Creek and East Brush Creek, climb up a small hill through the aspens as the trail takes a more northerly direction. Part way up this hill, the East Brush Creek Trail (see Route 58) leaves the Middle Brush Creek Trail. Stay on the latter as it climbs up through the Middle Brush Creek Valley. Teocalli Ridge (see Route 56) will be on your left.

After traveling about four miles the trail makes a sharp switchback up and right and leaves the Middle Brush Creek Trail and valley. Use Mount Teocalli as a landmark and read your map carefully here to ensure staying on the Pearl Pass route rather than traveling too far up Middle Brush Creek into Cumberland Basin.

By skiing up the Pearl Pass Trail as marked on the USGS *Pearl Pass* map, you will head up a small drainage and end up in the basin on the west side of Carbonate Hill. Study your map carefully and you will see that the trail climbs to a broad saddle a little north of the Carbonate Hill summit (57-C). Many people have mistaken this saddle for Pearl Pass and skied down into East Brush Creek only to find themselves back on the trail they had skied up! To avoid this mistake, simply follow the trail on the USGS map as it

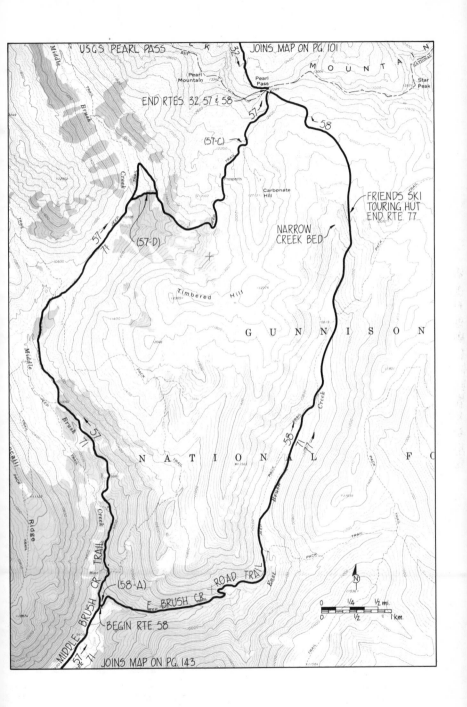

contours in a northerly direction from the saddle, then climbs a short way up to the pass. Return via the same route or ski to the Ashcroft roadhead (Route 32), or ski down East Brush Creek and back to Middle Brush Creek to make a nice loop (Route 58).

Avalanche notes: Large but infrequent slides run over the trail in the central part of the Middle Brush Creek Valley. Where the trail switchbacks up out of the Middle Brush Creek Valley, a major slide threatens the route. If you do not like staring into the muzzle of a loaded gun, simply take to the trees on the right (57-D) (to the south of the trail). The other spot with problems is the traverse to the pass from the saddle north of Carbonate Hill. This area may have been stabilized by wind compaction. If it hasn't been, the alternative is to climb one of the rocky ribs that will take you over the east ridge of Pearl Mountain.

58 East Brush Creek to Pearl Pass

Difficulty: Advanced
Time: Probably an overnight
Distance: 11 miles
Elevation gain: 3,800 feet
Starting elevation: 9,000 feet
USGS 7.5 minute map: Pearl Pass

Map—page 145

Though not as popular as the Middle Brush Creek route to Pearl Pass, this route is as good. It might have a bit more avalanche danger because it is difficult, though not impossible, to skirt the slide runouts in the narrow East Brush Creek Valley. This route will undoubtedly become more popular now that the Friends Hut (see Route 77) is complete.

To ski this route to Pearl Pass, follow Middle Brush Creek (see Route 57) to the 9,440-foot elevation, where the road climbs a small hill into Middle Brush Creek (58-A). This is just past the three ponds on the map. A short distance up this hill the East Brush Creek Road trail forks to the right. There is a sign here, but it may be covered by snow. From this intersection ski the East Brush Creek Road trail, as marked on the USGS *Pearl Pass* map, for about 1 ½ miles in an easterly direction, then stay on the road trail as it turns north. Continue up the East Brush Creek Valley, but deviate from the packtrail marked on the USGS map in order to avoid the runouts from the avalanche slopes on the west side of the valley.

At the 10,800-foot level, the USGS *Pearl Pass* map shows the packtrail leaving the valley and heading toward Crystal Peak. Do not use this trail. Follow a better route by staying in the valley for another ¼ of a mile, then doing a climbing traverse to the north through an evergreen forest on the east side of the creek. This traverse follows a poorly marked trail to the Friends Hut (see Route 77), which sits atop the tree-studded knoll at timberline (11,400 feet) just to the east of the last confluence in East Brush Creek. This traverse up to the Friends Hut is an important part of the route because it avoids the narrow gully the creek flows down.

Once at the Friends Hut, use Star Peak and the Pearl Pass saddle as landmarks. Stay on the easterly side of the basin and climb a series of ribs and shelves to just below the pass. Switchback or kick steps up the last hundred feet to the road cut that leads a few hundred feet up to the actual pass summit.

Return is via the same route. Take care to follow the east side of the basin, and stay out of the narrow gully that holds the creek from 11,600-foot level to 11,000 feet. For the route toward Aspen from the pass summit, see Route 32.

Avalanche notes: Beware of the slopes on the west side of the East Brush Creek drainage. Pay attention to the slopes coming off the ridge between Pearl Pass and Star Peak—these are usually wind scoured, but can occasionally be loaded and dangerous.

CHAPTER SIX

Routes from Independence Pass Road

When the Independence Pass portion of Colorado Highway 82 is open in the spring and late fall, it provides access to some of the most convenient high-altitude touring in the Elks. In the winter, the road is closed about five miles out of Aspen. The snow-covered road makes a good winter tour (Route 60), and there are several other tours that start from the portion of the road that is always open. Parking along the road is no problem in the winter, since there are places where the plow widens the road for that purpose. To find out the status of the road closure, call the Colorado Highway Patrol (see Appendix C).

59 Difficult Campground and Difficult Trail

Difficulty: Novice
Time: 2 to 5 hours
Distance: Varies with route
Elevation gain: Varies with route
Starting elevation: 8,000 feet
USGS 7.5 minute map: Aspen

Map—page 150

Difficult Campground is a good touring area 2 ½ miles up the Independence Pass Road (Highway 82) out of Aspen (see Route 60). Park in the area just off the road near the sign announcing the campground. The sign can be a bit hard to spot since it is set back from the road. A more prominent sign visible from the main road says White River National Forest. If you pass this sign, you have driven too far.

Ski down the snow-covered campground access road for about ¾ of a mile into the campground, where there are numerous snow-covered roads and trail cuts. The more ambitious can take the

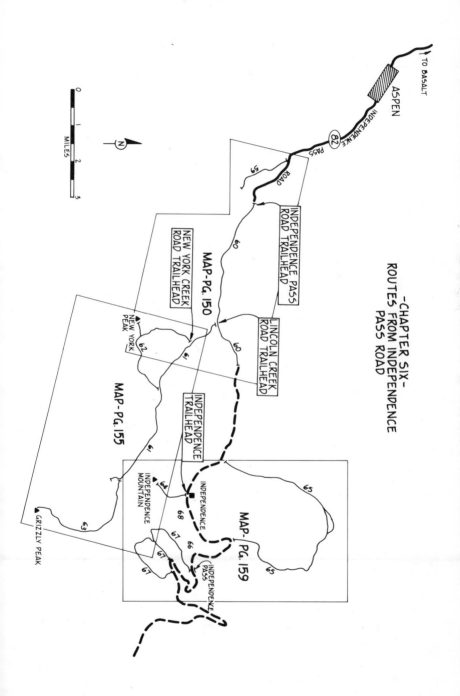

-CHAPTER SIX-
ROUTES FROM INDEPENDENCE
PASS ROAD

0 1 2 3
MILES

N

TO BASALT

ASPEN

INDEPENDENCE PASS

82

PASS ROAD

59

60

INDEPENDENCE PASS
ROAD TRAILHEAD

NEW YORK CREEK
ROAD TRAILHEAD

MAP-PG. 150

LINCOLN CREEK
ROAD TRAILHEAD

NEW
PEAK

NEW YORK

62

61

60

MAP-PG. 155

INDEPENDENCE
TRAILHEAD

61

INDEPENDENCE
MOUNTAIN

64

INDEPENDENCE

65

68

GRIZZLY PEAK

63

67

66

MAP-PG. 159

67

67

INDEPENDENCE
PASS

65

149

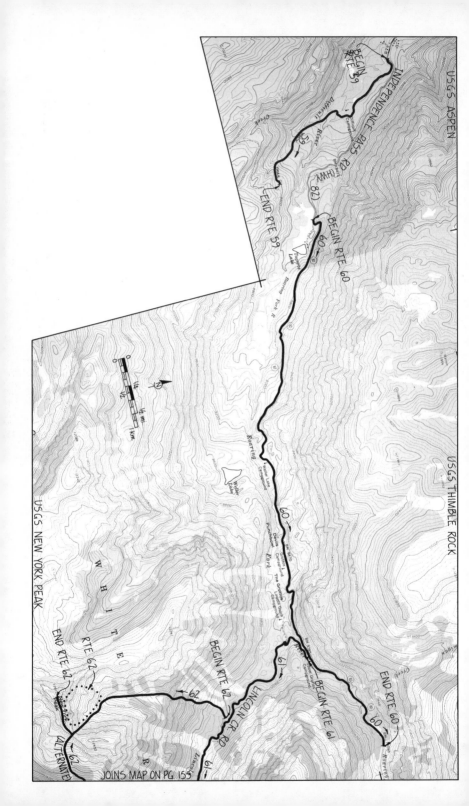

BEGIN RTE 39

INDEPENDENCE PASS RD (HWY 82)

END RTE 59

BEGIN RTE 60

Roaring Fork R.

Difficult Campground

Lincoln Gulch Campground

Portal Lake

Weller Lake

Lincoln Gulch Campground

Roaring Fork R.

Lost Man Campground

Lincoln Creek Campground

Portal Campground

Lincoln Lake Campground

60

61

62

Devils Punchbowl
The Grottos
Lincoln Gulch
Campground

BEGIN RTE 62

END RTE 62

RTE 62

W H I T E

LINCOLN CR RD

BEGIN RTE 61

END RTE 60

BEGIN RTE 61

ALTERNATE 62

JOINS MAP ON PG 155

N
0
¼   ½ mi.
½   1 km.

Skiing into Mountain Boy Gulch from Independence Pass. (Lou Dawson photo)

Difficult Trail up the valley out of the campground. To find this trail, ski down the road into the campground and cross the green closure gate next to an outhouse. To your right, you will see another green closure gate. Leave the main road here, cross the closure gate, and ski an obvious trail that takes you to a footbridge across the creek. Cross the bridge and climb up on to the flat shelf on this (west) side of the creek. Ski up the valley a short distance to a steep hill that begins in a grove of evergreens. The trail climbs this hill up a steep, narrow cut through the trees. It is skiable for about a mile after this point, then climbs some less than enjoyable switchbacks into the Difficult Creek drainage; do not bother with this part of the trail.

Avalanche notes: There is no danger in the campground, and the Difficult Trail is safe up to the switchbacks.

60   Independence Pass Road

Difficulty: Novice
Time: Depends on distance traveled
Distance: Depends on distance traveled
Elevation gain: Depends on distance traveled
Starting elevation: 8,600 feet
USGS 7.5 minute maps: Aspen, New York Peak, Thimble Rock

Map—page 150

As indicated at the beginning of the chapter, the Independence Pass Road is closed in the winter, and this closed portion makes a good ski tour. The snow is usually packed by snowmobiles, and you may encounter a few of these raging beasts. Remember that this is one of the few places they are allowed at this end of the valley.

Avalanche notes: The valley is safe up to the large paths that come off Green Mountain (about five miles past the road closure). After this point there are numerous runouts crossing the road. Take normal precautions, and travel the more dangerous section only during times of stability.

61   Lincoln Creek Road

Difficulty: Novice
Time: 3 hours to Grizzly Reservoir
Distance: 6 miles from the road fork to Grizzly Reservoir
Elevation gain: 1,000 feet
Starting elevation: 9,785 feet
USGS 7.5 minute maps: New York Peak, Independence Pass

Maps—pages 150 and 155

In the spring when it finally opens, this road off the Independence Pass Road provides access to Routes 62 and 63. In the late fall and early winter, when the Independence Road is still open, the Lincoln Creek Road itself makes an excellent ski trip to Grizzly Reservoir because the road is relatively flat and usually packed down by snowmobiles.

The road is easy to find. It is about 9 ½ miles up the Independence Pass Road out of Aspen (3 ½ miles past the winter road closure). The turnoff is well signed, and begins by crossing the

Skiing in the Independence Pass area, with La Plata Peak in the background. (Michael Kennedy photo)

Roaring Fork over a bridge with a Forest Service road closure gate.

Avalanche notes: There is little danger for the first three miles, although beyond that some large chutes threaten the road from the south side of Green Mountain.

62   New York Peak

Difficulty: Advanced
Time: 6 hours round trip
**Distance: First route: 4 miles round trip. Second route: slightly
    longer than 4 miles round trip.**
Elevation gain: 2,000 feet
Starting elevation: 9,800 feet
USGS 7.5 minute map: New York Peak

Map—page 155

Because of its accessibility and short length, this excellent spring ski descent is a gem for those still acquainting themselves with summit ski descents. Once the Lincoln Creek Road is open in the spring (see Route 61), it is easy to climb two excellent routes to the summit.

For the first route, drive about a mile down the Lincoln Creek Road (see Route 61) and park there. This should put you near the stream that comes down from the northeast bowl of the peak. Bushwhack up the northwest side of the stream. When you break out of the timber into the bowl, head in a southerly direction to the obvious saddle between the summit and Point 12,450 on the map. From this saddle, follow the ridge to the summit. The ski route either follows the ascent route or takes the classic gully that drops down the north face from the summit.

For the second route, drive about two miles farther along the Lincoln Creek Road to the point where a small sign announces New York Creek on the right. Follow the road trail shown on the USGS *New York Peak* map leading from this sign up New York Creek. In about a mile leave the trail and climb up the southeast shoulder of New York Peak to the saddle described above. From there, take the ridge to the summit. Use either of the ski descent routes described above.

Avalanche notes: Climb and ski this mountain during safe spring conditions.

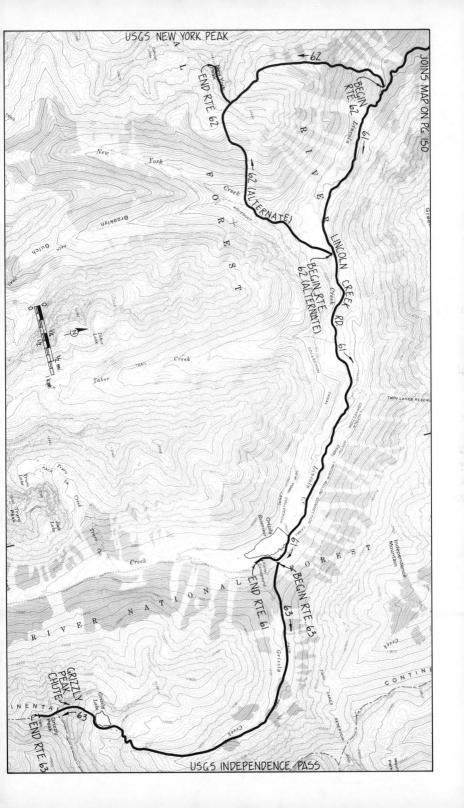

END RTE 62

BEGIN RTE 62

62

61

62 (ALTERNATE)

BEGIN RTE 62 (ALTERNATE)

LINCOLN CREEK RD

61

GRIZZLY PEAK CHUTE

END RTE 61

BEGIN RTE 63

63

END RTE 63

A pocket slab avalanche is a dangerous trap for the unwary. (Lou Dawson photo)

63 Grizzly Peak Chute

Difficulty: Advanced
Time: 8 hours round trip from Grizzly Reservoir
Distance: 9 miles round trip
Elevation gain: 3,400 feet
Starting elevation: 10,537 feet
USGS 7.5 minute map: Independence Pass

Map—page 155

Grizzly Peak is just 10 feet under fourteener status. If you stand on the rock cairn on the summit, your head will be in the rarefied air that only about 53 other peaks in Colorado enjoy.

To climb the peak, drive five miles up the Lincoln Creek Road (see Route 61). This should put you just past the Grizzly Reservoir dam and directly up the hill from a group of buildings. Park here and take the trail marked on the map that leads to Grizzly Lake. The beginning of this trail is marked by a Forest Service sign that says Grizzly Lake Trail 1990. Once at the lake you will see the beautiful snow gully that breaks the north side of Grizzly Peak. Climb directly up the gully, then follow a short ridge to the summit.

The ski descent is via the impressive gully. With a maximum

angle of 45 degrees, it does not classify as extreme skiing if conditions are good, but at times there are large ice patches that make skiing difficult. A careful assessment of conditions is important for a safe trip. Most parties use ice axes and crampons for the ascent.

Avalanche notes: This high mountain gully is safe for skiing only after the spring snowpack has consolidated.

64 Independence Mountain

Difficulty: Intermediate
Time: 5 hours round trip
Distance: 4 miles round trip
Elevation gain: 1,900 feet
Starting elevation: 10,800 feet
USGS 7.5 minute map: Independence Pass

Map—page 159

This is the classically shaped little peak that rises to the south of the ghost town of Independence on the Independence Pass Road (see Route 60). The good downhill skiing is in the east bowl, skied from the summit. Excellent runs can be had in both spring and late fall, while the Independence Road is still open for access. To climb the peak, park near the ghost town and ski up the north flank to the north ridge, then to the summit. The route is simple.

Avalanche notes: In spring the bowl should be skied early in the morning on frozen snow. In the fall, watch out for a dangerous buildup of a TG crystal layer.

65 Lost Man Trail

Difficulty: Intermediate
Time: 5 hours
Distance: 7 miles
Elevation gain: 1,200 feet
Starting elevation: 11,506 feet
USGS 7.5 minute maps: Independence Pass, Mount Champion

Map—page 159

This is a good loop trip to do in late fall or spring, when the Independence Pass Road is open. Eighteen miles up the Independ-

Climbing in the Independence Pass area. (Gnurps photo)

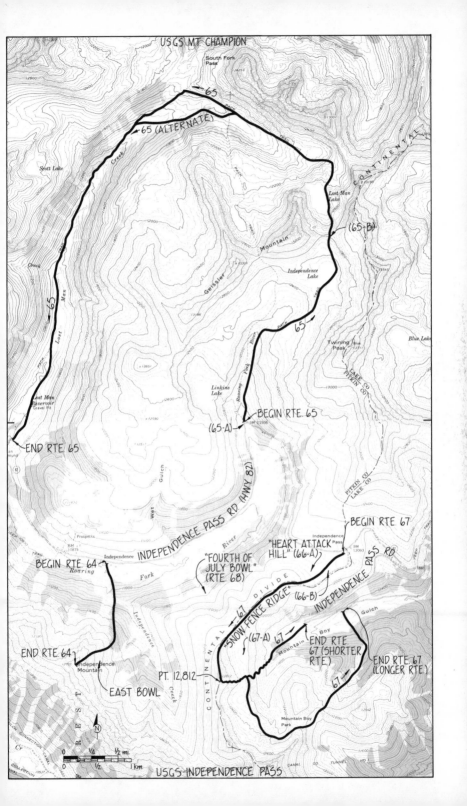

ence Pass Road (Highway 82, see chapter introduction) out of Aspen, a hairpin turn (65-A) begins the last switchback up to the pass. Leave your car at the parking area here, and ski the drainage to the north that leads to a small pass (65-B) separating Lost Man Lake and Independence Lake. From the pass, ski down past Lost Man Lake, then down Lost Man Creek to Lost Man Reservoir, where the trail intersects Independence Pass Road.

With foresight you can bring two cars and leave one at the reservoir trailhead as you pass it on your way to the hairpin trailhead. If you do not leave a car at the reservoir, it is usually no problem for a person with skis to hitchhike up the road and pick up the group's vehicle at the hairpin (65-A).

Avalanche notes: For the most part this is a safe route—the few avalanche paths that cross the trail are easily skirted. Take care not to ski into pocket slabs while going over the pass (65-B).

66   Heart Attack Hill and Environs (Independence Pass Summit)

Difficulty: Novice
Time: Varies with activity
Distance: ¼ mile from the bottom to the top of the hill
Elevation gain: 200 feet
Starting elevation: 12,093 feet
USGS 7.5 minute map: Independence Pass

Map—page 159

About ½ mile from the actual summit of Independence Pass (see chapter introduction), on the Aspen side, there is an excellent little ski hill south of the road (66-A). This is called "Heart Attack Hill" by those suffering from altitude-induced angina. Heart Attack Hill is an excellent place for downhill ski practice when the Independence Pass Road is open in late fall or spring. Because the hill is covered by smooth tundra, a thin snow cover will provide good skiing. From Heart Attack Hill to the summit of the pass is a large area of gently rolling terrain (66-B). This is a good place for the beginning cross-country skier, as well as the nordic racer who wants to set an early season track.

Avalanche notes: This area is safe because of the generally low angles.

Skiing into Mountain Boy Gulch. Snowfence Ridge is above. (Lou Dawson photo)

67 Snow Fence Ridge and Mountain Boy Gulch

Difficulty: Intermediate
Time: 4 hours
Distance: Approximately 4 miles, depending on route
Elevation gain: 700 feet
Starting elevation: 12,093 feet
USGS 7.5 minute map: Independence Hill

Map—page 159

From Heart Attack Hill (see Route 66), you can follow the beautiful ridge to the southwest (the continental divide) called the "Snow Fence Ridge." It has this distinctive name because of the

Rube Goldberg snow fences built on the crest of the ridge so that drifts of snow might accumulate for the summer's supply of meltwater. These fences are being removed. The ridge to Point 12,812 and back makes a nice tour, or you can drop down several good ski runs on the southeast side of the ridge (67-A). These runs will take you down into Mountain Boy Gulch. Once in the Gulch you can ski down to the Independence Pass Road and hitch back to the pass summit.

You can make a longer tour by skiing to Mountain Boy Park, contouring to the 12,200-foot saddle, then skiing north down the intermittent stream that drops into Mountain Boy Gulch.

Avalanche notes: The various ski routes off the Snow Fence Ridge are avalanche paths, and can only be skied in total safety in spring. If you ski the Mountain Boy Park route, be careful of the slopes leading to the saddles, which can be loaded with snow.

68   Fourth of July Bowl

Difficulty: Advanced
Time: 1 to 2 hours, depending on transportation for the trip back up the road to Independence Pass
Distance: 2 miles
Elevation gain: 400 feet
Starting elevation: 12,093 feet
USGS 7.5 minute map: Independence Pass

Map—page 159

On the northwest side of the Snow Fence Ridge (Route 67) is a beautiful bowl that takes you down to a lower point on the Independence Pass Road. The bowl earned the name "Fourth of July" because of the nearby town of Independence, founded July 4, 1879, and because the bowl holds snow so well it is skiable late into July.

To reach the top of the bowl for a ski descent, simply walk along Snow Fence Ridge from Heart Attack Hill (Route 66). The various descents into the bowl will be on your right.

Avalanche notes: Most of the terrain in the bowl should be skied only in safe spring conditions.

The last leg to Pearl Pass. A safer route follows a more direct line just to the left of the higher skier. (Lou Dawson photo)

CHAPTER SEVEN

Three Ski Routes Connecting Aspen and Crested Butte

One of the best ways to do a long tour in the Elks is to connect the towns of Aspen and Crested Butte with a route across the mountains. Since the spine of the Elks runs east-west and Crested Butte and Aspen lie north and south of each other, it is only logical that skiing between the towns would be a superb mountaineering experience. It is; and the following three routes are best.

These routes usually require a night out in the wilds, yet they can be done in a day by experienced parties. The Pearl Pass Route (71) has even been completed several times in under five hours. All the routes pass through avalanche terrain and should only be traveled

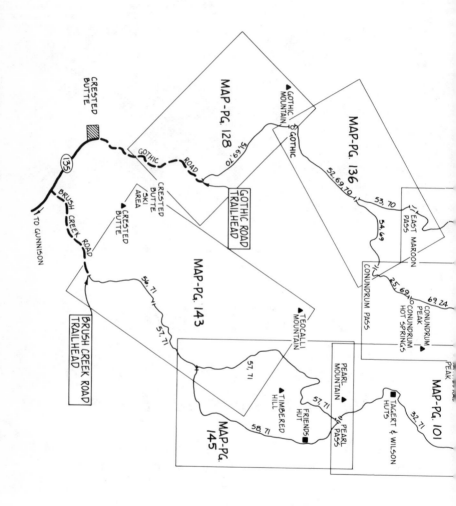

CRESTED BUTTE

135

TO GUNNISON

BRUSH CREEK ROAD

GOTHIC ROAD 57,69,70

MAP-PG. 128

GOTHIC MOUNTAIN

GOTHIC

MAP-PG. 136

52,69,70

53,70

54,69

EAST MAROON PASS

GOTHIC ROAD TRAILHEAD

CRESTED BUTTE SKI AREA

CRESTED BUTTE

MAP-PG. 143

56,71

57,71

BRUSH CREEK ROAD TRAILHEAD

CONUNDRUM PASS

25,69,70 CONUNDRUM HOT SPRINGS

69,24 CONUNDRUM PEAK

PEAK

TEOCALLI MOUNTAIN

57,71

PEARL MOUNTAIN

MAP-PG. 101

TIMBERED HILL

FRIENDS HUT

57,71

PEARL PASS

TAGERT & WILSON HUTS

32,71

58,71

MAP-PG. 145

164

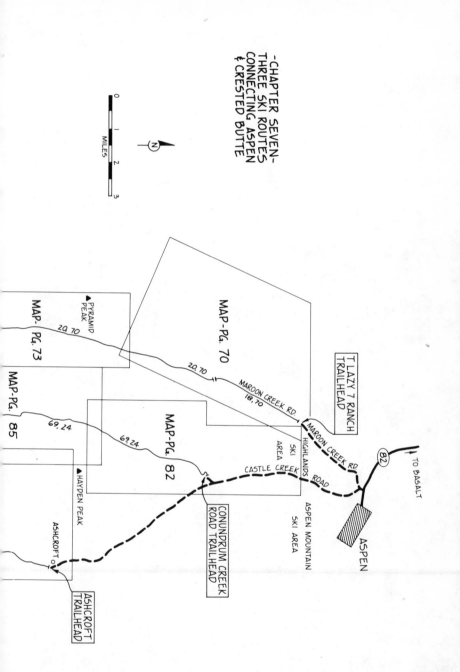

- CHAPTER SEVEN -
THREE SKI ROUTES
CONNECTING ASPEN
& CRESTED BUTTE

MILES
0 1 2 3

N

MAP-PG. 70

MAP-PG. 73

▲ PYRAMID PEAK

29, 70

20, 70

MAROON CREEK RD.

18, 70

T LAZY 7 RANCH TRAILHEAD

MAROON CREEK RD.

82

TO BASALT

MAP-PG. 85

69, 24

MAP-PG. 82

69, 24

CASTLE CREEK

HIGHLANDS ROAD

SKI AREA

ASPEN MOUNTAIN SKI AREA

ASPEN

CONUNDRUM CREEK ROAD TRAILHEAD

▲ HAYDEN PEAK

ASHCROFT

ASHCROFT TRAILHEAD

Sastrugi patterns indicate wind-compacted snow. (Michael Kennedy photo)

during times of relatively low risk. The guide services in both Aspen and Crested Butte can provide experienced guides for the trip if you feel that you are not skilled enough to do it safely on your own (see Appendix C).

Once you have skied one of the routes between the two towns, the problem is the return to your point of origin. This is best accomplished by a flight on one of the numerous charter airlines operating out of Aspen and Crested Butte. Enthusiastic skiers can make their own way back over the mountains if they have time.

The route descriptions below have been simplified with references to route descriptions in other chapters that combine to make the tour. Where these descriptions are written in reverse order from your travel direction, simply follow the directions for return (this will usually mean reversing the same route).

69 Conundrum Pass Route between Aspen and Crested Butte

Difficulty: Advanced
Time: 2 days with a night out
Distance: 25 miles
Elevation gain: 4,500 feet from the Aspen side; 3,500 feet from the Crested Butte side
Starting elevations: Aspen, 8,600 feet; Crested Butte, 9,000 feet
USGS 7.5 minute maps: Gothic, Maroon Bells, Hayden Peak, Aspen

Maps—pages 82, 85, 128, and 136

This is probably the most difficult and dangerous of the three routes described here. You will have to spend one night out, preferably at the hot springs. In midwinter deep snow conditions, the trip can take more than one night. It is a toss-up as to which direction the route is best traveled. Coming from Aspen makes the hot springs a more logical place to spend a night, but coming from Crested Butte eliminates the long slog up the Conundrum Valley. See Routes 24, 25, 51, 52, and 54 for descriptions that combine to make this tour.

Avalanche notes: Take care not to let the attraction of the hot springs get in the way of good judgment. If you are coming from the Aspen side, for example, and are caught in a storm, it might be prudent to wait a day for the snow to stabilize a bit.

70   East Maroon Pass Route between Aspen and Crested Butte

Difficulty: Advanced
Time: 2 days plus one night out
Distance: 20 miles
Elevation gain: 2,500 feet from the Crested Butte side; 3,700 feet from the Aspen side
Starting elevations: Aspen (T Lazy 7 Guest Ranch), 8,236 feet; Crested Butte (Ski Area), 9,400 feet
USGS 7.5 minute maps: Gothic, Maroon Bells, Highland Peak

Maps—pages 70, 73, 128, and 136

This is the simplest of the routes between Crested Butte and Aspen. It might, on the average, be better from the Crested Butte side because that exposure on East Maroon Pass is more likely to be stabilized by wind compaction. When skiing avalanche terrain, it is always better to use safe slopes for the ascent and the less safe for the descent. See Routes 18, 20, 51, 52, and 53 for the descriptions that combine to make this trip.

Avalanche notes: See route descriptions listed above.

71   Pearl Pass Route between Crested Butte and Aspen

Difficulty: Advanced
Time: Two days, plus one night out
Distance: 21 miles
Elevation gain: 3,200 feet from the Aspen side; 3,800 feet from the Crested Butte side
Starting elevations: Aspen (Ashcroft), 9,498 feet; Crested Butte, 9,000 feet
USGS 7.5 minute maps: Crested Butte, Pearl Pass, Hayden Peak

Maps—pages 101, 143, and 145

This is the most popular route between the two towns. For the Crested Butte side of the pass, begin on Route 56 and continue on either Route 57 or 58; for the Aspen side use Route 32. If you are coming from the Crested Butte side, camp at timberline below Carbonate Hill, or at the Friends Hut (see Route 77). Coming from the Aspen side, stay at the Friends Hut or at the Tagert Hut (see

Tagert Hut. (Lou Dawson photo)

Route 72). As with the Conundrum Route (69), there is no best direction to ski this trip. On either side there are potential avalanche slopes, although all these slopes can be avoided if one is willing to make the extra effort to scramble up some rock ribs and deviate into timbered areas. If you are skiing from Aspen it is probably better to ski into East Brush Creek (see Route 58). If you are skiing from Crested Butte, take care on the Aspen side of the pass to turn to the northwest and ski through Pearl Basin and into the Castle Creek drainage. Do not make the common and potentially disastrous mistake of being tempted by the attractive slopes that lead from the summit of the pass directly north and down into the Cooper Creek drainage, since the creek necks down into a dangerous, avalanche-exposed chute.

Avalanche notes: See the route descriptions listed above that combine to describe this trip.

CHAPTER EIGHT

Alfred Braun Hut System and Friends Hut

The United States Ski Educational Foundation operates and maintains five shelter huts in the central Elks between Aspen and Crested Butte. For those skiing on the Aspen side of the range, they are well placed to serve as shelter for several ski trips, including Pearl Pass to Crested Butte (Route 71) and a multiday trip connecting all the huts. The huts are usually booked well in advance, and since they are used by reservation only by one party at a time, there can be a shortage of available nights—especially on weekends. So plan your trip and reserve your nights far in advance. This can be done by contacting the hut committee chairman (see Appendix C).

The Friends Hut (Route 77), though not officially a part of the Braun Hut System, ties in well with the Braun Huts. It is a good stopping place while traveling between Crested Butte and Aspen (see Chapter 7). For information on how to make reservations, call the Forest Service in Gunnison or Crested Butte or write the Friends Hut (see Appendix C).

72 Tagert and Wilson Huts

Difficulty: Intermediate
Time: 5 hours
Distance: 6 miles
Elevation gain: 2,000 feet
Starting elevation: 9,498 feet
USGS 7.5 minute maps: Hayden Peak

Map—page 101

These huts, built next to each other, can accommodate several large groups. They are useful as an overnight stop on the way to Crested Butte (Route 71). There is quite a bit of enjoyable ski terrain in Pearl Basin above the huts, and they make a good base

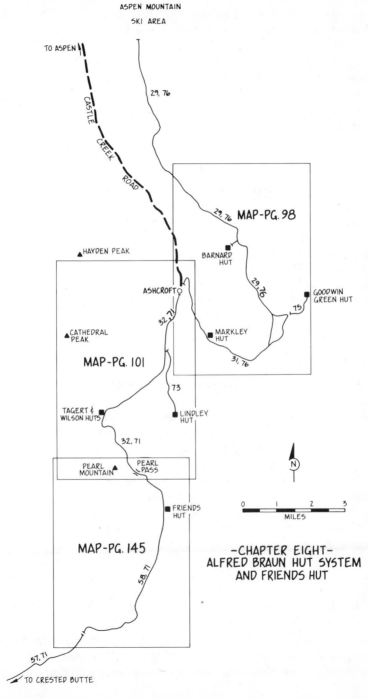

ASPEN MOUNTAIN
SKI AREA

TO ASPEN

29, 76

CASTLE CREEK ROAD

29, 76 MAP-PG. 98

HAYDEN PEAK

BARNARD HUT

29, 76

ASHCROFT

GOODWIN GREEN HUT

75

32, 71

CATHEDRAL PEAK

MARKLEY HUT

MAP-PG. 101

31, 76

73

TAGERT & WILSON HUTS

LINDLEY HUT

32, 71

N

PEARL MOUNTAIN

PEARL PASS

FRIENDS HUT

0   1   2   3
MILES

MAP-PG. 145

—CHAPTER EIGHT—
ALFRED BRAUN HUT SYSTEM
AND FRIENDS HUT

58, 71

57, 71

TO CRESTED BUTTE

171

camp for a ski-climb of Castle Peak (Route 33). The Tagert and Wilson huts are fairly easy to find, but take the time and effort to read your map carefully—don't be lulled into carelessness by the short distance to the huts. To reach the huts, follow Route 32 up the Pearl Pass Road for ¼ mile past the turnoff onto the Montezuma Basin Road. The huts can be spotted on the hillside east of the stream (see map in text for exact location).

Avalanche notes: See Route 32.

73   Lindley Hut

Difficulty: Novice
Time: 3 hours
Distance: 4 ½ miles from Ashcroft
Elevation gain: 1,000 feet
Starting elevation: 9,480 feet
USGS 7.5 minute map: Hayden Peak

Map—page 101

This hut is reached by following the Castle Creek Road up the valley from the Ashcroft road closure (see Route 32). Continue up the main valley. Do not head up the Pearl Pass Road—there may be a sign at the junction that clarifies the routes. The snow-covered road will lead to a gated bridge near the green buildings of the Ashcroft Transfer Station (73-A), where iron ore from the mountain above is transferred into trucks to be hauled down the Castle Creek Road during the summer. Cross the bridge and ski up the Iron Mine Road (the obvious road cut into the east side of the valley). Follow this road for about 1 ¼ miles past the bridge to the first switchback (73-B). From the apex of the switchback, contour south into the valley for several hundred yards, then drop down to the hut hidden in a dense grove of evergreens (see map in text for exact location). Be careful not to ski too far up the road or to contour from the switchback too far upvalley from the hut.

Avalanche notes: Just before the Ashcroft Transfer Station there are several slopes that threaten the trail from the west side of the valley. The Iron Mine Road is exposed to some paths up to the east, which slide infrequently (see Route 32). Take normal precautions, and travel this route during times of lower hazard.

On the way to Tagert Hut. (Lou Dawson photo)

74 Markley Hut

Difficulty: Novice
Time: 3 hours
Distance: 2 ½ miles
Elevation gain: 800 feet
Starting elevation: 9,480 feet
USGS 7.5 minute map: Hayden Peak

Map—page 98

This is the easiest to reach of the huts, and is one of the best ones for beginning ski tourers to enjoy. To reach the hut, take Route 31 out of Ashcroft for about 2 ½ miles up Express Creek. Because the hut is down to the right in a grove of trees, it is not visible from the road, and the turnoff is nondescript (see map in text). There is usually a small sign marking the turnoff. A common mistake is to ski past the hut, but careful map reading will prevent this.

Avalanche notes: See Route 31.

There may *be a sign in the Ashcroft valley where the trail forks to the hut. (Lou Dawson photo)*

75   Goodwin Green Hut

Difficulty: Advanced
Time: 8 hours from Ashcroft; 6 hours from Barnard Hut
Distance: 8 miles from Ashcroft; 5 miles from Barnard Hut
Elevation gain: 2,000 feet from Ashcroft; 650 feet from Barnard Hut
Starting elevations: Ashcroft, 9,480 feet; Barnard Hut, 11,480 feet
USGS 7.5 minute maps: New York Peak, Hayden Peak

Map—page 98

This and the Barnard Hut (Route 76) are the only official ski cabins that give a real taste of ski mountaineering in the Elks. These two huts are located within a day's travel of one another, and can be used for shelter on a Richmond Hill tour or from Ashcroft (see Routes 29, 31).

To reach the Goodwin Green Hut from Ashcroft, follow Route 31 to the Gold Hill area. Contour around the south side of Gold Hill using the same route as the packtrail marked on the USGS *New York Peak* map. Take the pass just to the east of Gold

Hill and ski down to the hut, taking care not to ski too low into the drainage. Return is via the same route. Or with good snow conditions you can ski a short way down into Difficult Creek, then to the west back onto Richmond Hill and out to civilization (see Routes 28, 29, 76).

Avalanche notes: See Route 31. Beware of slopes on the north and east sides of Gold Hill.

To reach the Goodwin Green Hut from the Barnard Hut (Aspen direction), follow Route 76 to the Barnard Hut. From there ski the jeep trail shown on the map, climbing up just to the east of McArthur Mountain. Continue to the south of McArthur up over another ridge and intersect the trail that heads around the south side of Gold Hill. Then follow this trail over the pass and ski down to the hut.

Avalanche notes: See above, and the second part of Route 76.

76 Barnard Hut

Difficulty: Advanced
Time: 10 hours from Ashcroft; 9 hours from the Sun Deck Restaurant
Distance: 9 miles from Ashcroft; 8 miles from the Sun Deck Restaurant
Elevation gain: 2,300 feet from Ashcroft; about 700 feet (depending on the exact route) from the Sun Deck Restaurant
Starting elevation: 9,480 feet (Ashcroft); 11,212 feet (Sun Deck Restaurant)
USGS 7.5 minute maps: Hayden Peak, New York Peak (from Ashcroft); Aspen, Hayden Peak (from the Sun Deck Restaurant)

Map—page 98

This is a truly beautiful ski cabin located in a spot with wonderful views and access to a variety of ski terrain. Of all the huts, it is the most difficult to find and has the longest approach routes. The hut lies in gently rolling, heavily timbered terrain with few obvious landmarks, and is not visible until you are within a few hundred feet of the small knoll where it sits. To be sure of finding this hut, you must be an excellent map reader; this means being able to use compass bearings as well as terrain recognition. There are two routes to the Barnard Hut: (1) from the Sun Deck Restaurant southward along Richmond Hill, and (2) from Ashcroft up Express Creek, then northward along Richmond Hill.

BARNARD HUT

Looking down at the Barnard Hut from McArthur Mountain. (Michael Kennedy photo)

To reach the Barnard Hut from the north end of Richmond Hill (this is the top of the Aspen Mountain Ski Area and the locale of the Sundeck Restaurant): travel to the top of the north end of Richmond Hill via either Route 28 or the Aspen Mountain ski lifts.

Once at the north end of Richmond Hill follow Route 29 southerly along the crest of Richmond Hill for about 5 miles to an open meadow at the head of McFarlane Creek (76-A). The road to this point may be packed by snowcats used by powder skiing guide services. Take care not to let cat trails mislead you.

From the head of McFarlane Creek the trail is difficult to find, and requires expert orienteering skills. Ski to the southeast along the westerly edge of the meadow (still using the trail marked on the USGS *Hayden Peak* map), then follow a road cut through the trees that leads down into the head of the West Difficult Creek drainage (76-B).

Once at the head of the West Difficult Creek drainage, take care not to drop too low. Follow the trail marked on the USGS *Hayden Peak* map as it parallels the creek and then climbs a hill in an easterly direction. On the top of the hill (76-C) you will break into another flat area where the USGS map shows a swamp.

From the swamp you must follow a confusing route that wanders in a southerly direction through a sparsely timbered area, then passes through a nondescript saddle at the 11,480-foot level (76-D). After the saddle the trail drops a bit and passes to the east of the hut, which is on a timbered knob about 200 yards to the west of the trail (see map in text for exact location).

This route is confusing, and many experienced mountaineers have wandered around Richmond Hill looking for this hut. The trick is to use compass bearings for positive landmark and route identification. And remember that a compass bearing will not work unless you know where you are.

For the return to Aspen Mountain Ski Area, reverse the above route. Take care to climb back up to Richmond Hill after the drop into the West Fork of Difficult Creek.

Avalanche notes: This route is fairly safe, but beware of small pockets on the different summits of Richmond Hill, and of dangerous chutes like the various McFarlane drainages, which drop off both sides of Richmond Hill.

To reach the Barnard Hut from Ashcroft, follow Route 31. Stick to the Express Creek drainage and climb to the top of the point at the head of the drainage. This point (76-E) is easily identified on the USGS map by the trail passing just to the east of

Friends Hut. (Lou Dawson photo)

the top. From the point take a compass bearing to identify McArthur Mountain to the north. Ski to the flat area (76-F) just to the east of the summit of McArthur (you are still on the official trail marked on the USGS *Hayden Peak* map). From there ski north down an obvious wide corridor through the timber (76-G). At the base of the corridor you will ski out into a large open area. Ski across it to the hut, which is hidden by the trees on the small knoll at the head of Fall Creek and just past the swampy area (76-H) shown on the USGS *Hayden Peak* map. Use your map and compass often while negotiating this route. For the return to civilization, ski the first route or reverse this one.

Avalanche notes: Once on Richmond Hill there is usually little danger because wind-scoured areas and compacted snow can be found for a safe route above timber. Much of the route crosses terrain too low angled for avalanches. See Route 31 for more information, and take the usual precautions.

77   Friends Hut

Difficulty: Advanced
Time: 9 hours from the Crested Butte side; 5 hours from the Tagert and Wilson huts on the Aspen side
Distance: 10 miles from the Crested Butte side; 4 ½ miles from the Tagert and Wilson huts
Elevation gain: 2,400 feet from the Crested Butte side; 1,500 feet from the Tagert and Wilson huts
Starting elevation: Ashcroft, 9,500 feet; Tagert and Wilson huts, 11,240 feet; Crested Butte side (Brush Creek roadhead), 9,000 feet
USGS 7.5 minute maps: Pearl Pass, Gothic, Hayden Peak

Maps—pages 101 and 145

To reach the Friends Hut from the Crested Butte side, begin on Route 56. Continue on Route 57 up Brush Creek, and then ski Route 58 up East Brush Creek. The hut is located at 11,400 feet just at timberline in the basin to the east of Carbonate Hill. It is in a grove of trees on the point several hundred yards to the east of the last confluence in East Brush Creek (see map in text). The hut may be difficult to find, especially when traveling from the Crested Butte side. There is a blazed trail in the dense timber below the hut, but the blazes may be covered by heavy snow.

To reach the hut from the Aspen side follow Route 32 to Pearl Pass. Then drop into East Brush Creek from Pearl Pass as described in Route 58.

The hut can also be reached from the Crested Butte side by skiing up to Carbonate Hill via Route 57, then down East Brush Creek Basin to the hut.

Avalanche notes: See Routes 57 and 58.

Skiing on the Tenth Mountain Trail; Gore Range in the distance. (Lou Dawson photo)

CHAPTER NINE

The Tenth Mountain Trail

For a number of years a traditional ski expedition for Vail and Aspen area residents has been the trip connecting the two towns. There are several alternative routes, involving varying degrees of difficulty, distance, and avalanche danger. In 1982 the Tenth Mountain Trail Association, a nonprofit organization, was formed to build huts on, make improvements to, and promote the safest and most enjoyable of these routes for the average nordic skier. This trail, known as the Tenth Mountain Trail, follows the foothills of the Sawatch Mountain Range from Aspen to Vail pass.

The Tenth Mountain Trail can be skied as a seven-to-ten-day expedition, or it can be done in segments, using the access roads and trailheads described below. The trail is described in sections

(Routes 78 through 90), from Aspen to Vail. Of course, the entire route—as well as individual sections—can be skied in either direction.

As of this writing, most of the trail already exists, though small sections of the official route are still subject to change. Three of the cabins proposed for the route—McNamara, Margy's and Estin huts (see Routes 78, 79 and 83)—already exist, but the other huts are now in the planning stages and should be built before 1989. Commercial accommodations exist in the Frying Pan Valley and at Lime Park, and Redcliff (see Appendix C for names and addresses). Elsewhere along the Tenth Mountain Trail, overnight skiers will have to camp. For the latest information on recommended routes and reserving space in huts or other accommodations, write to the Tenth Mountain Trail Association (see Appendix C).

The terrain along the trail is generally safe from avalanches, but a few areas should be avoided during times of high hazard. The routes use a combination of snow-covered roads, open parks, and Forest Service trails. Some sections of the trail are poorly marked and may not follow a definitive cut. Navigation can be tricky in open parks and on snow-covered logging roads, and trail markers may be missing altogether or hidden by deep snow. Travel carefully, with frequent map checks, and always be sure of your return route.

Access Roads and Trailheads

Eleven roads and their corresponding trailheads provide access and egress along the Tenth Mountain Trail, permitting skiers to join or leave it at convenient intervals. These accesses make a variety of shorter trips possible and can save valuable time in case of emergency. Directions for each road and trailhead are given below, in sequence from Aspen to Vail. Their locations are shown both on the overview map of the Tenth Mountain Trail and on the topographic maps accompanying Routes 78 through 90.

Upper Hunter Creek Trailhead and Hunter Creek Parking Area (USGS 7.5 minute map *Aspen*). There is no parking at the Upper Hunter Creek Trailhead. So either have someone drop you off, or park at the Hunter Creek Trail Parking Area (see below) and walk to the trailhead.

To reach the Upper Hunter Creek Trailhead by car, drive north on Mill Street from the stoplight next to the Jerome Hotel in central Aspen. Drive down the Mill Street Hill and over a bridge that crosses the Roaring Fork River. After crossing the bridge, take a

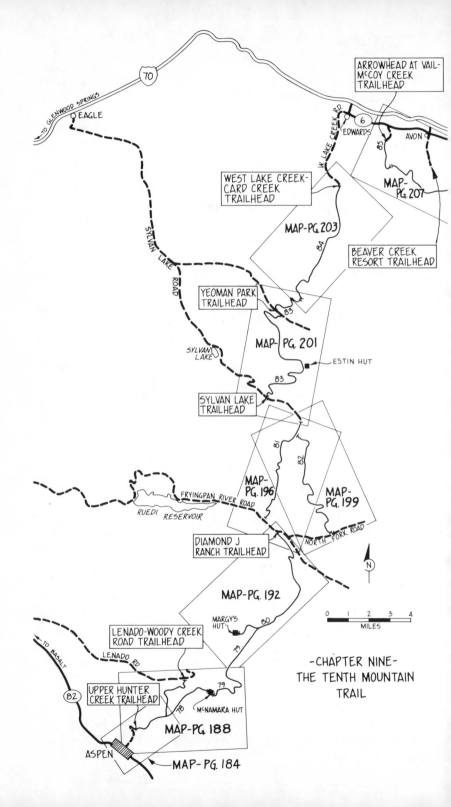

ARROWHEAD AT VAIL-
MᶜCOY CREEK
TRAILHEAD

70

TO GLENWOOD SPRINGS
EAGLE

6
EDWARDS
AVON
85

W. LAKE CREEK RD.

WEST LAKE CREEK-
CARD CREEK
TRAILHEAD

MAP-
PG. 207

MAP-PG. 203

84

BEAVER CREEK
RESORT TRAILHEAD

SYLVAN LAKE ROAD

YEOMAN PARK
TRAILHEAD

83

MAP- PG. 201

SYLVAN
LAKE

ESTIN HUT

83

SYLVAN LAKE
TRAILHEAD

81
82

MAP-
PG. 196

MAP-
PG. 199

FRYINGPAN RIVER ROAD

RUEDI RESERVOIR

NORTH FORK ROAD

N

DIAMOND J
RANCH TRAILHEAD

0 1 2 3 4
MILES

MAP-PG. 192

MARGY'S
HUT

80

-CHAPTER NINE-
THE TENTH MOUNTAIN
TRAIL

TO BASALT

LENADO-WOODY CREEK
ROAD TRAILHEAD

LENADO RD.

79

82

UPPER HUNTER
CREEK TRAILHEAD

79

McNAMARA HUT

78

MAP-PG. 188

ASPEN

MAP- PG. 184

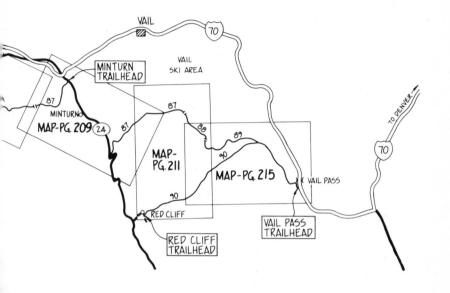

left curve and stay on the main road; this is the Red Mountain Road. Follow the Red Mountain Road for a little over a mile up steep hills and switchbacks to the large flat area where the well-signed Red's Road heads left and right. Do not turn onto Red's Road, just continue north toward the top of Red Mountain. (The roads from here to the trailhead are private; they have been used for access since they were built, but be aware that this could change at any time.) The road will continue to climb up and to the right, then around a switchback. Just before the end of the road there is a gate on the right with a sign welcoming hikers and horses. The dirt road past this gate is the highest access to Hunter Creek.

The Hunter Creek Parking Area is at the Hunter Creek water treatment plant. To find it, follow the road directions for the Upper Hunter Creek Trailhead. Bust just before the second hairpin turn on Red Mountain Road (you will be about halfway up through the

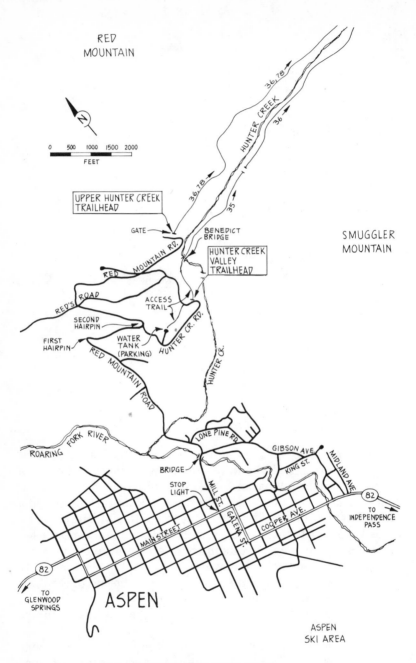

RED
MOUNTAIN

N

0 500 1000 1500 2000
FEET

HUNTER CREEK

36,78

36

35

36,78

SMUGGLER
MOUNTAIN

UPPER HUNTER CREEK
TRAILHEAD

GATE

RED MOUNTAIN RD.

BENEDICT
BRIDGE

HUNTER CREEK
VALLEY
TRAILHEAD

RED'S ROAD

RED

ACCESS
TRAIL

SECOND
HAIRPIN

FIRST
HAIRPIN

WATER
TANK
(PARKING)

HUNTER CR. RD.

HUNTER CR.

RED MOUNTAIN ROAD

ROARING FORK RIVER

LONE PINE RD.

GIBSON AVE.

KING ST.

MIDLAND AVE.

BRIDGE

STOP
LIGHT

MILL ST.

GALENA ST.

COOPER AVE.

82

TO
INDEPENDENCE
PASS

MAIN STREET

82

TO
GLENWOOD
SPRINGS

ASPEN

ASPEN
SKI AREA

DETAIL OF HUNTER CREEK TRAILHEADS.
FOR TOPOGRAPHICAL INFORMATION SEE
MAP ON PAGE 107.

residential section), take a turn to the right. There may be a sign at this turn that says: "Hunter Creek Trail Parking" and points to the right with an arrow. Follow the road a short way and watch for a water tank on the left. Take the driveway that leads behind the tank to a parking turnaround. This is the highest public parking on Red Mountain. From here, walk back to the Red Mountain Road and continue uphill to the Upper Hunter Creek Trailhead.

Lenado-Woody Creek Road and Trailhead (USGS 7.5 minute maps *Thimble Rock, Aspen*). Drive to Lenado by taking the Woody Creek Road that turns off Highway 82, six miles west of Aspen. Drive the Woody Creek Road 2.1 miles to an unsigned hard right, and turn onto the Lenado Road (this turn is just past the Woody Creek Trailer Park). Follow the Lenado Road eight miles to Lenado.

Drive through Lenado (a small group of buildings on both sides of the road) to the snowplow turnaround that ends the plowed portion of the road. Park here and ski the road to a bridge over Woody Creek. To ski to Spruce Creek, leave the snow-covered road at this bridge and ski up the south side of Woody Creek. Cross the creek where there are good snow bridges, and be careful to identify the Woody Creek-Spruce Creek confluence (see Route 79).

Diamond J Ranch Trailhead (USGS 7.5 minute maps *Ruedi, Meredith, Red Creek*). The Diamond J Ranch is a focal point for tours in the Frying Pan River drainage. To reach the Diamond J Ranch, drive to the town of Basalt on Highway 82 (the road between Aspen and Glenwood Springs). Take the main street through the town—it will become the Frying Pan River Road. Follow it 26 miles to the Diamond J Ranch on the south side of the road.

Sylvan Lake Trailhead (USGS 7.5 minute maps *Fulford, Crooked Creek, Red Creek, The Seven Hermits*). To reach this trailhead, take the Eagle exit off I-70 29 miles west of Vail Resort. Drive through Eagle following a well-signed route to the Sylvan Lake Road beginning on the south side of town. There is a good sign at the start of the Sylvan Lake Road. From Eagle, follow the road 16 miles to Sylvan Lake. Parking is no problem in the Sylvan Lake area.

Yeoman Park Trailhead (USGS 7.5 minute maps *Fulford, Crooked Creek, Red Creek, The Seven Hermits*). Drive to the town of Eagle and the beginning of the Sylvan Lake Road (for directions see *Sylvan Lake Trailhead* above). From Eagle follow the Sylvan Lake Road about 10 miles to a well-signed fork. Take the left fork and drive six miles to Yeoman Park. You can park at the snowplow turnaround.

West Lake Creek-Card Creek Trailhead (USGS 7.5 minute maps *Grouse Mountain, Edwards*). Drive I-70 to the Edwards exit, 13 miles west of Vail Resort. Take the Edwards exit and drive south for a short distance across the Eagle River to a stop sign on Old Highway 6. Drive right (west) from the stop sign 0.6 mile along Old Highway 6 to the poorly signed Lake Creek Road turnoff to the south. (There may be a sign on a bus shelter at this intersection.) Follow Lake Creek Road 1.9 miles to a well-signed intersection, where the road splits. The left fork is the East Lake Creek Road; the right fork is the West Lake Creek Road. Follow the right (west) fork three miles to a parking area where a switchback takes a hard turn to the left. Park here. The Card Creek drainage trail follows the obvious snow-covered road that heads south from this parking area.

Arrowhead at Vail-McCoy Creek Trailhead (USGS 7.5 minute map *Edwards*). Take the Edwards exit off I-70, about 13 miles west of Vail Ski Resort. Cross the Eagle River, then take a left at a stop sign onto Old Highway 6. Follow it east for about two miles to the Arrowhead at Vail development near the McCoy Creek, Eagle River confluence. Park at the development (ask permission for overnight parking).

Beaver Creek Resort Trailhead (USGS 7.5 minute maps *Edwards, Grouse Mountain*). Take the Avon exit off I-70, 9.25 miles west of Vail Resort. Park in the large parking area and take a shuttle bus to the ski slopes.

To reach the Arrowhead at Vail-McCoy Creek section (Route 85) of the Tenth Mountain Trail, hike up the ski area or ride Chair 12 to the warming shack for the McCoy Park Touring Center. Ski the set track in McCoy Park to its northernmost point into the McCoy Creek drainage.

To reach the Beaver Creek Resort-Minturn Section (Route 86) of the Tenth Mountain Trail, ride lifts or ski up to the Chair 7 terminus and restaurant at Spruce Saddle, within the Beaver Creek Ski Area. Gain the Tenth Mountain Trail here, as it descends Spruce Saddle Meadow, traverses to Meadow Mountain, then continues to the Minturn trailhead and beyond (see Route 87).

Minturn Trailhead (USGS 7.5 minute map *Minturn*). From I-70, take the Minturn exit onto Highway 24 (about five miles to the west of Vail Resort). Just after turning off you will see a green Forest Service road closure gate next to a white house on the

McNamara Hut. (Lou Dawson photo)

southwest side of the road. This gate marks the trailhead for Meadow Mountain.

For the Two Elk Creek route (87) out of Minturn, either walk or drive through Minturn and continue south on the highway to a bridge where the highway crosses over the Eagle River. Park here. Walk the railroad tracks back down the valley about ¾ of a mile to the Two Elk Creek drainage.

Vail Pass Trailhead (USGS 7.5 minute map *Vail Pass*). Drive on I-70, 14 miles to the east of Vail Resort. Park at the large parking area just east of the overpass near the summit of the pass. The start of the Shrine Pass Road is well signed and very well used.

Red Cliff Trailhead (USGS 7.5 minute map *Minturn*). To reach Red Cliff, take the Minturn exit off I-70 (about five miles west

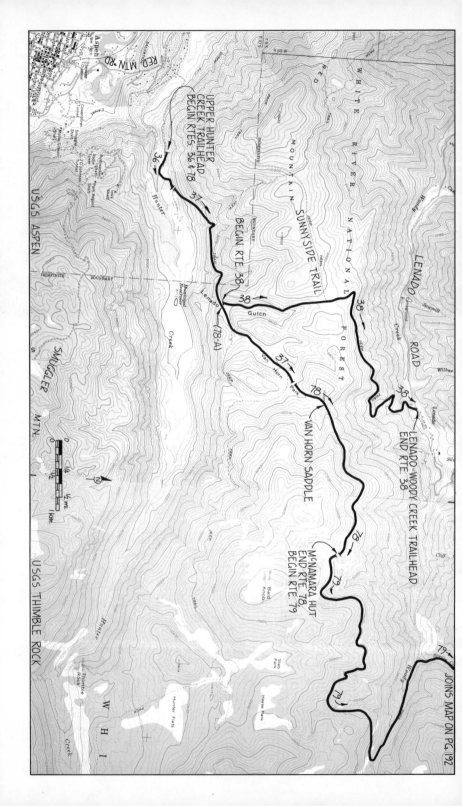

USGS ASPEN

USGS THIMBLE ROCK

RED MTN. RD.

Aspen

SMUGGLER MTN.

UPPER HUNTER CREEK TRAILHEAD BEGIN RTES. 36 & 78

36

37

BEGIN RTE. 38

SUNNYSIDE TRAIL

WHITE RIVER NATIONAL FOREST

MOUNTAIN

Lenado

38

Gulch

(78-A)

37

Van Horn Park

78

LENADO ROAD

38

LENADO-WOODY CREEK TRAILHEAD END RTE. 38

VAN HORN SADDLE

McNAMARA HUT END RTE. 78 BEGIN RTE. 79

78

79

Bald Knob

Slab Park

Horse Park

Hunter Flats

Thimble Rock

W H I

79

79

JOINS MAP ON PG. 192

N

0   ¼   ½ mi.

0   ¼   ½   1 km.

Hunter   Creek

Hunter

Creek

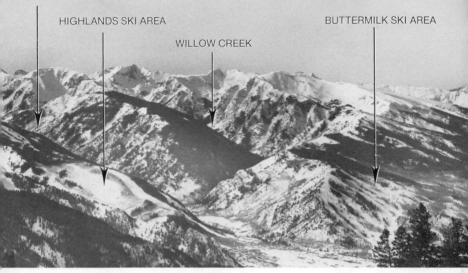

View to the west from Bald Knob. (Lou Dawson photo)

of Vail Resort) onto Highway 24. Drive through Minturn and over Battle Mountain to Red Cliff. If you are driving from the south of Denver, go to Leadville and take Highway 24 from there to Red Cliff.

78 Aspen to McNamara Hut via Hunter Creek and Van Horn Park

Difficulty: Intermediate
Time: 5 hours
Distance: 6 miles
Elevation gain: 2,000 feet
Starting elevation: About 8,000 feet, depending on route
USGS 7.5 minute maps: Aspen, Thimble Rock

Maps—pages 184 and 188

The McNamara Hut is a beautiful cabin nestled in a pine forest at the base of Bald Knob, with sleeping room for fifteen people. Reservations are required—for information contact the Tenth Mountain Trail Association (see Appendix C).

View toward Margy's Hut from Bald Knob. (Lou Dawson photo)

To begin the trip to the McNamara Hut from Aspen, ski into the Hunter Creek Valley from the Upper Hunter Creek trailhead. From there, follow the dirt road, which shortly leads to a well-defined trail cut through brush and trees on the north side of the valley. Once in the valley, ski the upper jeep road to Van Horn Park. To find this road, locate the barbed wire fence that heads up the hill north from the big white teepee at the lower end of the valley. The road begins on the up-valley side of the fence, just uphill from the prominent green steel gate.

Ski this road as it climbs northeast for about 1¾ miles to a large flat open area (78-A). Just before this open area the Lenado trail splits off to the north (see Route 38). Take care not to get on the Lenado trail, but ski easterly across the open area, then head up a gulch to the left (north), after which you will soon break out of the trees into Van Horn Park. Because the roads in this area are numerous and for the most part unsigned, be sure to read your map carefully. Ski to the upper (north) end of the park, then to the small saddle (Van Horn Saddle) just to the east of Point 10,097.

From Van Horn Saddle begin an easterly contour on a cleared, well-marked trail that gradually climbs through timber on the north side of Bald Knob to the McNamara Hut at the 10,440-foot level next to an intermittent stream (see map in text for exact location). This is not a difficult trail to follow, but be careful to contour from Van Horn Saddle and not to drop to the north into the dense timber and steep terrain of the Woody Creek drainage.

To reverse the route, take care to get on the proper trail from the cabin. This can be difficult after a heavy storm or when there have been many skiers in the area; a compass bearing can help. Stay on the trail as it contours and drops gently to Van Horn Saddle. Again, be careful not to drop into the Woody Creek drainage.

Avalanche notes: This is a very safe route. Take care on the steeper open slopes in Van Horn Park.

79 McNamara Hut to Margy's Hut via Spruce Creek

Difficulty: Intermediate
Time: 7 hours
Distance: 7 ½ miles
Elevation gain: 1,700 feet
Starting elevation: McNamara Hut, 10,440 feet; Margy's Hut, 11,200 feet
USGS 7.5 minute maps: Thimble Rock, Meredith

Maps—pages 188 and 192

Margy's Hut is another beautiful ski cabin similar in design to the McNamara Hut. For reservation information contact the Tenth Mountain Trail Association (see Appendix C).

The trail, which is well marked and cleared, contours from the McNamara Hut (Route 78) in an easterly direction about 1½ miles, then drops into the Woody Creek drainage and follows to the north side of Woody Creek for about a mile down the valley to its confluence with the Spruce Creek drainage. Spruce Creek is easy to identify because it is the only main drainage near this point.

Ski up the Spruce Creek drainage about 3½ miles to Sawmill Park. Continue your careful map reading, and from the lower westerly end of Sawmill Park begin a long climbing traverse back

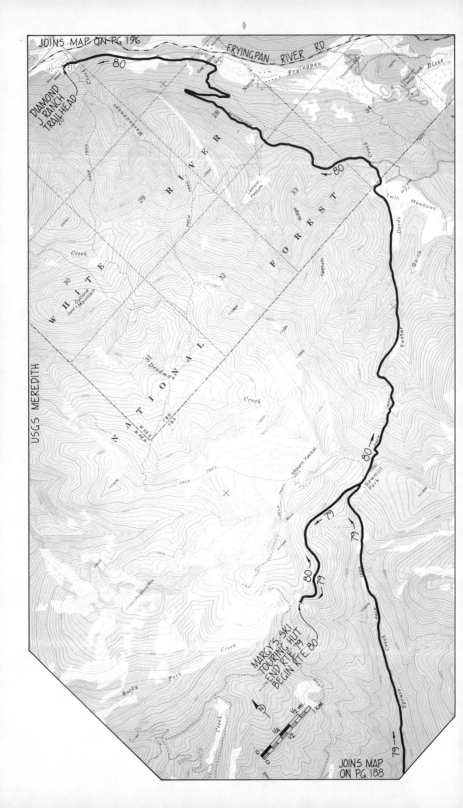

FRYINGPAN RIVER RD.

Fryingpan

34

DIAMOND
J RANCH
TRAILHEAD

80

28

R
I
V
E
R

Lamont
Pasture

33

Twin
Meadows

W
H
I
T
E

29

30

Creek

Cyclone
Mountain

32

ridge

F
O
R
E
S
T

Teetum

Deeds

Gulch

Foster

80

Deadman

Creek

N
A
T
I
O
N
A
L

80

Creek

Sawmill
Park

Mount Yeckel

79

PACK   TRAIL

79

80   79

Creek

Fork

Rocky

MARGY'S SKI
TOURING HUT
END RTE 79
BEGIN RTE 80

N

½ mi.

km.

¼

½

0

Creek

Spruce

79

Margy's Hut. (Michael Kennedy photo)

in a southwesterly direction 1¼ miles to Margy's Hut, located at 11,200 feet on the ridge dividing Rocky Fork Creek from Spruce Creek (see map in text for exact location). This section of the trail can be quite confusing, and though it is marked and cleared it is still possible to stray into dense timber and end up on the ridge above or below the hut. Careful map reading and trail identification will prevent this.

To reverse the route use the same trail, taking special care to stay on the traverse to Sawmill Park. The small town of Lenado may be used as a roadhead and trailhead for Woody Creek.

Avalanche notes: This route is fairly safe, though there is the possibility of sluffing on the steep banks in the Woody Creek and Spruce Creek drainages.

80 Margy's Hut to Diamond J Ranch via Twin Meadows

Difficulty: Intermediate
Time: 8 hours from Diamond J Ranch; 7 hours to Diamond J Ranch
Distance: 9 miles
Elevation gain: 2,900 feet from the Diamond J Ranch
Starting elevation: 11,200 feet
USGS 7.5 minute map: Meredith

Map—page 192

From Margy's Hut take the trail back to Sawmill Park (Route 79). From the north end of Sawmill Park ski the packtrail marked on the USGS *Meredith* map. This trail leads through heavy timber and occasional clearings down Foster Gulch and Deeds Creek to the obvious open area called Twin Meadows.

The Lime Creek Road trailhead. (Lou Dawson photo)

From the north end of Twin Meadows ski a short way north and intersect the road that traverses in a northwesterly direction and drops into the Frying Pan River drainage. Near the intersection of this road with the plowed main road take a left while still on the south side of the Frying Pan River, about where the word "gate" is on the USGS map, and ski 1¼ miles down the valley to the Diamond J Ranch.

To reverse the route, leave the Diamond J Ranch and ski or drive up the Frying Pan Valley to the road from Twin Meadows. Ski to Twin Meadows, then take care to stay on the trail up Deeds Creek, then up Foster Gulch to Sawmill Park. From Sawmill Park take the trail that traverses over to Margy's Hut (Route 79). See "Diamond J Ranch Trailhead" for information about the Diamond J Ranch.

Avalanche notes: This is a very safe route.

81 Diamond J Ranch to Crooked Creek Reservoir via Lime Creek Road

Difficulty: Intermediate
Time: 8 hours
Distance: 8 miles
Elevation gain: 1,000 feet
Starting elevation: 8,300 feet
USGS 7.5 minute maps: Meredith, Crooked Creek Pass

Map—page 196

The simplest though not the most direct route to Crooked Creek Reservoir follows the Lime Creek Road in a northerly direction from the Frying Pan Road. The Diamond J Ranch is on the Frying Pan Road (see "Diamond J Ranch Trailhead").

The Lime Creek Road turns off the Frying Pan Road just about one mile down the valley from the Diamond J Ranch (25 miles up the valley from Basalt). The turn is marked by a sign that says "Eagle 32 miles." The road may or may not be plowed for a short way. Take care not to get stuck while parking.

From your parking place, ski up the Lime Creek Road as it winds up several switchbacks and through lovely aspen forests. In several miles you'll break out into the large treeless area called Lime Park. Here it is necessary to read your map carefully and perhaps use a compass bearing to cross Lime Park and hit the

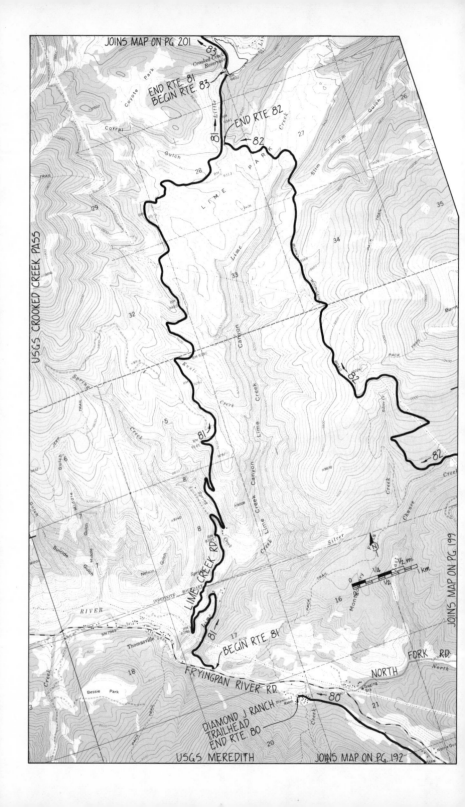

JOINS MAP ON PG. 201

END RTE 81
BEGIN RTE 83

83

Crooked Creek Reservoir

Coyote Park

Corral

Gulch

81

82

END RTE 82

Little

Creek

27

26

Slim

Jim

Gulch

28

29

LIME

PARK

Lime

33

Lime

Creek

34

35

32

Mystic

Creek

Lime

Canyon

81

82

Spring

Creek

5

Lime

Creek

82

Creek

Jeep

Gulch

6

LIME

PARK

ROAD

7

8

Silver

Nelson

Gulch

Silver Cr.

Silver Cr.

Chavez

Creek

Suicide

Gully

81

BEGIN RTE 81

16

Mont.

TN

FS

N

1/4 1/2 mi.

0 1/4 1/2 1 km.

RIVER

Thomasville

17

FRYINGPAN RIVER RD.

Bessie Park

18

FORK RD.

NORTH

North

80

DIAMOND J RANCH
TRAILHEAD
END RTE 80

21

20

JOINS MAP ON PG. 192

JOINS MAP ON PG. 199

USGS CROOKED CREEK PASS

*Fractures like this indicate snow instability and avalanche danger.
(Michael Kennedy photo)*

small drainage that the road follows to the reservoir. There is good camping in the trees around Crooked Creek Park. There may be a commercial ski touring operation here that can provide accommodations at the cabins by Crooked Creek Reservoir, and the Tenth Mountain Trail Association has proposed a hut for this area (send inquiries to the Tenth Mountain Trail Association—see Appendix C.)

To reverse the route use the Lime Creek Road, taking care to find your way across Lime Park.

Avalanche notes: This is a very safe route.

82 Diamond J Ranch to Crooked Creek Reservoir via Burnt Mountain Road

Difficulty: Intermediate
Time: 9 hours
Distance: 9 miles
Elevation gain: 1,700 feet from Diamond J Ranch; 900 feet from Crooked Creek Reservoir
Starting elevation: Diamond J Ranch, 8,300 feet
USGS 7.5 minute maps: Meredith, Nast, Crooked Creek Pass

Map—page 199

This alternate route between the Diamond J Ranch Trailhead and Crooked Creek Reservoir follows the snow-covered Burnt Mountain Road. It is a bit more difficult than the Lime Creek Road (Route 81).

From the Diamond J Ranch, car shuttle ½ mile up the valley on Frying Pan Road to its intersection with the North Fork Road (marked with a sign for "Elk Wallow Camp Ground").

Take a left on to the North Fork Road and drive for about two miles to the point where the USGS *Nast* map shows the Burnt Mountain Road leaving the North Fork Road. There is a sign at this intersection. Parking here can be a problem, so have someone drop you off.

Ski up the Burnt Mountain Road 5½ miles to its high point, then down into Lime Park. The best landmark for this section is the powerline the road passes under a number of times. Once in Lime Park, read your map carefully as you ski across Lime Park then

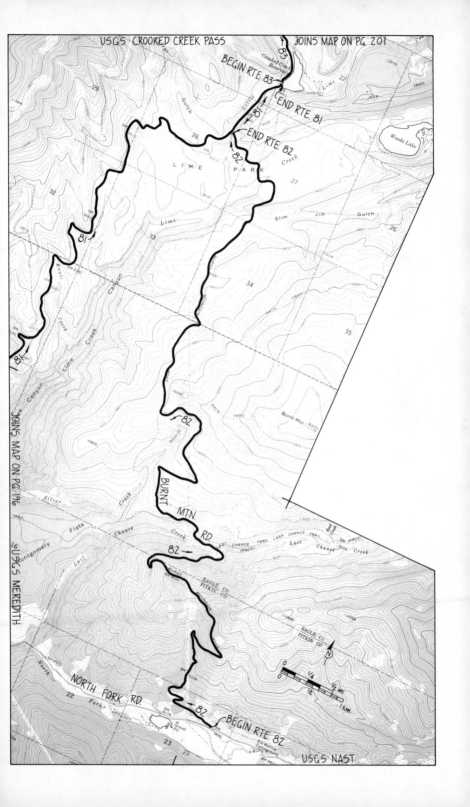

Signs indicating the Burnt Mountain Road trailhead. (Lou Dawson photo)

join up with Route 81 and ski Little Lime Creek to Crooked Creek Reservoir.

To reverse the route, follow Little Lime Creek from Crooked Creek Reservoir down into Lime Park. Read your map carefully, cross Lime Park, and intersect the Burnt Mountain Road. Follow the Burnt Mountain Road to the Frying Pan Valley and the Diamond J Ranch.

Avalanche notes: This is a very safe route. Take care not to ski into Lime Canyon.

83   Crooked Creek Reservoir to Fulford via Hat Creek and Fulford Road

Difficulty: Intermediate
Time: 10 hours
Distance: 12 miles
Elevation gain: 1,700 feet from Crooked Creek; 1,200 feet from Fulford
Starting elevation: 9,400 feet
USGS 7.5 minute maps: Crooked Creek Pass, Fulford

Map—page 201

From Crooked Creek Reservoir ski the road through Crooked Creek Park to Crooked Creek Pass. There is a good egress route

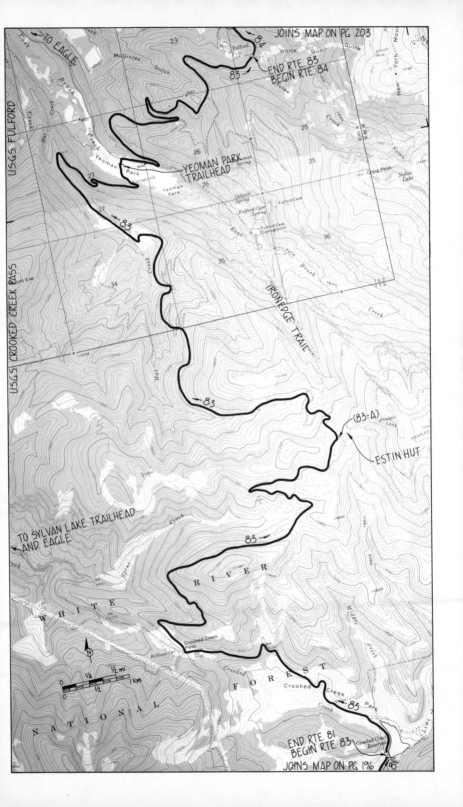

JOINS MAP ON PG. 203

TO EAGLE

McGinley   Gulch

23

Fulford   White   Quail   Gulch

84

END RTE 83
BEGIN RTE. 84

83

U.S.G.S. FULFORD

25

YEOMAN PARK
TRAILHEAD

Yeoman
Park

YEOMAN PARK
TRAILHEAD

26

Yeoman
Park

25

Craig Peak

Nolan
Lake

27

Galesatic
Spring

Fulford Cave
Spring   Fulford Cave

83

Fulford Cave
Campground

34

36

36

U.S.G.S. CROOKED CREEK PASS

IRONEDGE TRAIL

Creek

83

(83-A)

Prospect
Lake

ESTIN HUT

TO SYLVAN LAKE TRAILHEAD
AND EAGLE

Creek

83

R I V E R

Middle

W H I T E

Billings Spr.

Crooked Creek
Pass

Crooked Creek

F O R E S T

N

0   ¼   ½ mi.
0   ½   1 Km.

Crooked   Creek

Crooked Creek

N A T I O N A L

Crooked   Creek

83

END RTE. 81
BEGIN RTE. 83

Crooked Creek
Reservoir

JOINS MAP ON PG. 196

here from the pass to Sylvan Lake via the road to Eagle (see "Sylvan Lake Trailhead"). Read your map carefully to identify the pass, since it's not immediately obvious. Leave the main road at Crooked Creek Pass and ski in a northerly direction up a logging road to the head of the Spine Creek drainage, then up to another indistinct pass that separates the Spine Creek drainage from the Hat Creek drainage. The Estin Hut is located several hundred yards east of here. From this pass (83-A) follow the Hat Creek drainage down to Yeoman Park, taking care to stay on the road in the lower portion of the Hat Creek drainage.

From Yeoman Park ski up the snow-covered main road to the small group of buildings called Fulford on the USGS map. There is a road plowed to Yeoman Park from the town of Eagle off I-70. This is a good egress route for an emergency, and good access for joining the route at this point. See "Sylvan Lake Trailhead" and "Yeoman Park Trailhead."

To reverse Route 84, take care to find the beginning of the Hat Creek Road out of Yeoman Park. In the Spine Creek drainage pay attention to staying on the high road to Crooked Creek Pass—it's all too easy to ski down into the lower portion of the Spine Creek drainage.

Avalanche notes: This is a very safe route, though there is always the possibility of bank sluffs on road cuts.

84 Fulford to Card Creek via Triangle Creek and Squaw Creek Saddle

Difficulty: Intermediate
Time: 8 hours
Distance: 6 miles
Elevation gain: 1,000 feet from Fulford; 2,000 feet from Card Creek Meadow
Starting elevation: 9,880 feet
USGS 7.5 minute maps: Fulford, Grouse Mountain

Map—page 203

From Fulford ski in a northerly direction up the main road for about a mile to its intersection with Triangle Creek. Leave the main road here and follow the trail (as marked on the USGS *Fulford* map) up the Triangle Creek drainage to the saddle at the 10,600-foot level (84-A) between map Points 10,862 to the west and

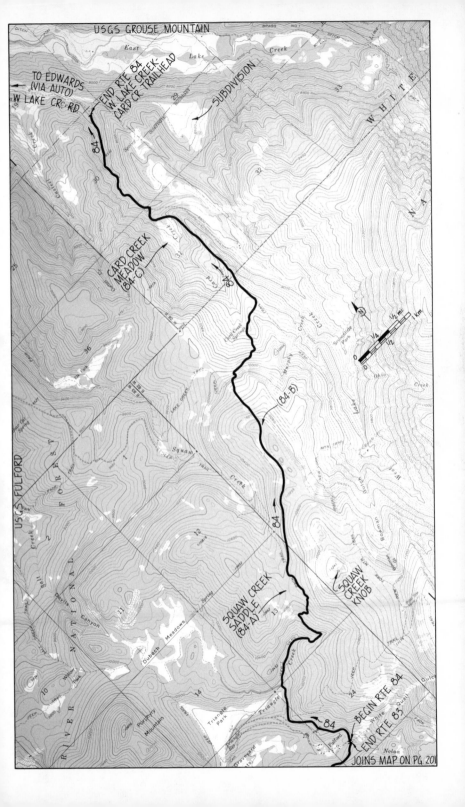

USGS GROUSE MOUNTAIN

TO EDWARDS
(VIA AUTO)
W LAKE CR. RD

END RTE 84
W. LAKE CREEK
CARD CR. TRAILHEAD

SUBDIVISION

84

CARD CREEK
MEADOW
(84-C)

84

(84-B)

USGS FULFORD

84

SQUAW CREEK
KNOB

SQUAW CREEK
SADDLE
(84-A)

84

BEGIN RTE 84
END RTE 83

84

JOINS MAP ON PG. 201

11,241 to the east. This saddle is called Squaw Creek Saddle, and Point 11,241 is known as Squaw Creek Knob.

Contour from Squaw Creek Saddle around the western side of Squaw Creek Knob, then ski north along the ridge coming off the north end of the knob. Descend this ridge to the north through open meadows to another saddle at the 10,720-foot level (84-B). This saddle divides the Card Creek and Lake Creek drainages. Navigation here can be a bit tricky because the route lies almost exactly on the border of the two maps and the trail passes through dense timber. Descend from the saddle through sparse aspen trees east into the Card Creek drainage, then follow Card Creek to the north to Card Creek Meadow (84-C). The two deserted cabins here

West Lake Creek–Card Creek Trailhead. The snow-covered road in the background is the beginning of the Card Creek to Fulford section of the Tenth Mountain Trail. (Lou Dawson photo)

are shown on the USGS *Grouse Mountain* map. There is good camping in this area. Consult the Tenth Mountain Trail Association about the possibility of a hut here (see Appendix C). From Card Creek Meadow, ski another mile down the jeep trail to the West Lake Creek Trailhead (see "West Lake Creek-Card Creek Trailhead").

To ski from Card Creek to Fulford, simply reverse these directions. Keep in mind that there is more climbing when traveling from Card Creek.

Avalanche notes: This is a safe route.

85   Arrowhead at Vail to Arrowhead Meadow

Difficulty: Intermediate
Time: 3 hours, in addition to access
Distance: 2 ½ miles
Elevation gain: 1,400 feet
Starting elevation: 7,400 feet
USGS 7.5 minute maps: Edwards, Grouse Mountain

Map—page 207

From the West Lake Creek (see Route 84) road and trailhead, drive north on the Lake Creek Road to Old Highway 6 east about three miles to the Arrowhead at Vail-McCoy Creek Trailhead. This driving is necessary to avoid private land through which a more direct ski route could travel. This ski route is in negotiation and could be worked out at any time—contact the Tenth Mountain Trail Association for current information (see Appendix C).

From the Arrowhead at Vail-McCoy Creek Trailhead, follow the trail (as marked on the USGS *Edwards* and *Grouse Mountain* maps) up the McCoy Creek drainage to Arrowhead Meadow.

Arrowhead Meadow is unnamed on the USGS *Grouse Mountain* map but is shown as the elongated meadow that extends from the 8,440-foot level to the 8,800-foot level. A small lake is shown at the north end of the meadow. There is good camping in this area. Contact the Tenth Mountain Trail Association about a possible hut here (see Appendix C). To reverse the route, reverse the above directions using the Diamond J Ranch Trailhead as your starting point.

Avalanche notes: This route is very safe.

Entering the lower (north) end of McCoy Park from Arrowhead Meadow. (Lou Dawson photo)

86 Arrowhead Meadow to Meadow Mountain via McCoy Creek and Beaver Creek Ski Area

Difficulty: Intermediate
Time: 7 hours
Distance: 7 miles
Elevation gain: 2,300 feet
Starting elevation: 8,740 feet
USGS 7.5 minute maps: Minturn, Grouse Mountain

Map—page 207

From Arrowhead Meadow (Route 85) ski a short way east into the McCoy Creek drainage. Ski up the south and west sides of McCoy Creek and cross the creek at the 9,600-foot level.

From the crossing, climb up through the west-facing glades to the east ridge of McCoy Park. Follow this ridge to the top of Chair 12 of the Beaver Creek Ski Area (see "Beaver Creek Resort Trailhead"). From the top of Chair 12, descend via Beano's Trace ski trail to the bottom of Chair 11. From the bottom of Chair 11 climb up the Dally and Cinch ski trails. Cross the ski area

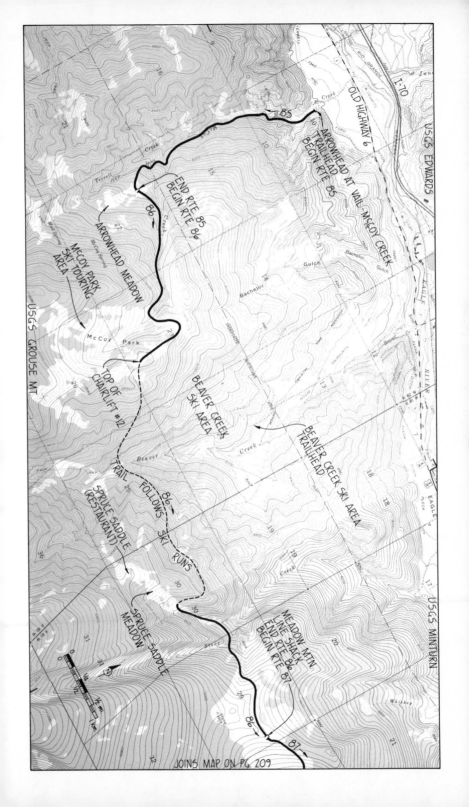

ARROWHEAD TRAILHEAD AT VAIL-MCCOY CREEK BEGIN RTE 85

END RTE 85 BEGIN RTE 86

ARROWHEAD MEADOW

McCOY PARK SKI TOURING AREA

McCOY PARK

TOP OF CHAIRLIFT #12

BEAVER CREEK SKI AREA

BEAVER CREEK SKI AREA TRAILHEAD

TRAIL FOLLOWS SKI RUNS

SPRUCE SADDLE (RESTAURANT)

SPRUCE SADDLE MEADOW

MEADOW MTN. LINE SHACK END RTE 86 BEGIN RTE 87

OLD HIGHWAY 6

I-70

USGS EDWARDS

USGS GROUSE MT.

USGS MINTURN

JOINS MAP ON PG. 209

boundary at the southernmost switchback on the Cinch Trail. It is helpful to pick up a trail map at the ski lift.

From the ski area boundary, traverse through the aspen trees to Spruce Saddle Meadow at 9,600 feet. Ski down Spruce Saddle Meadow and into the pine woods at the bottom. From here traverse to the east, and ski into the Stone Creek drainage at the 9,200-foot level. Climb out of the Stone Creek drainage onto a bench on the west side of Meadow Mountain. Follow this bench to the Meadow Mountain Line Shack. This is the building marked at the 9,740-foot level on the USGS *Minturn* map.

To reverse the route, reverse the preceding directions and simply climb Spruce Saddle Meadow to Spruce Saddle in the Beaver Creek Ski Area. The stretch from the Line Shack to the ski area can be complicated by dense timber, so read your map carefully to avoid problems here.

There is good camping in the trees above the Line Shack. Contact the Tenth Mountain Trail Association about a hut here (see Appendix C).

Avalanche notes: This is a safe route, but be aware of potential bank sluffs on the steep sides of Stone Creek.

87 Meadow Mountain-Two Elk Creek-Pete's Bowl

Difficulty: Intermediate
Time: 6 hours, in addition to driving time
Distance: 7 miles
Elevation gain: 1,680 feet
Starting elevation: 8,000 feet
USGS 7.5 minute maps: Minturn, Red Cliff

Maps—pages 209 and 211

From the Meadow Mountain Line Shack (Route 86), ski down and to the east for about two miles down the nonoperational Meadow Mountain ski area to Highway 24 (see "Minturn Trailhead"). Drive or walk Highway 24 to the parking spot for Two Elk Creek.

From the Two Elk Creek parking spot, follow the east side of the Eagle River Back about ¾ of a mile to the Two Elk Creek drainage. Ski the trail up the drainage as marked on the USGS *Minturn* and *Red Cliff* maps.

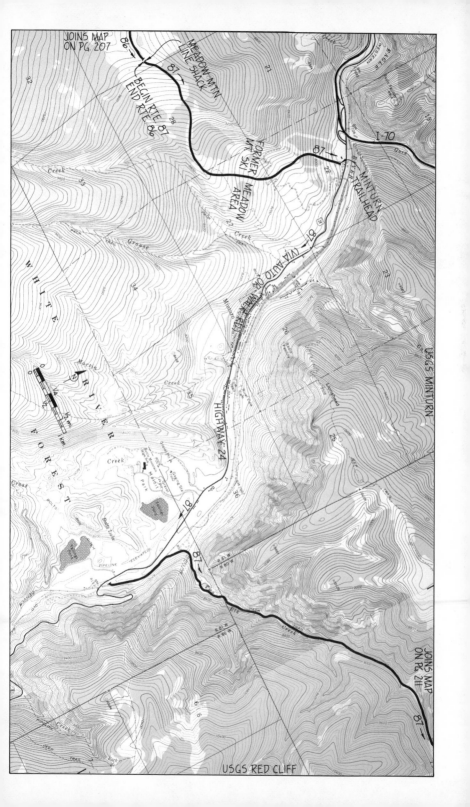

JOINS MAP
ON PG. 207

MEADOW MTN
LINE SHACK

86

87

BEGIN RTE 87
END RTE 86

28

FORMER
MT. MEADOW
SKI
AREA

21

I-70

87

MINTURN
BEAR TRAILHEAD

87 (VIA AUTO OR. MTN. RD.)

23

Creek

Creek

Creek

Grouse

W H I T E

Martin

R I V E R

Creek

35

34

F O R E S T

Creek

HIGHWAY 24

0   ¼   ½ mi
0   ¼   ½ Km

87

PARK

PIPELINE

36

26

25

87

87

JOINS MAP
ON PG. 211

87

USGS MINTURN

Cross

Creek

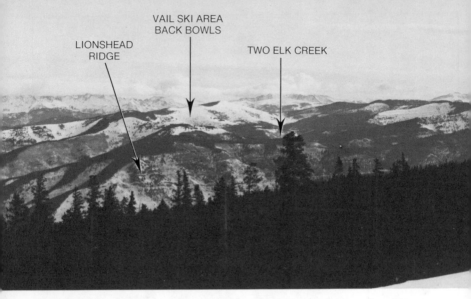

LIONSHEAD RIDGE

VAIL SKI AREA BACK BOWLS

TWO ELK CREEK

View from Beaver Creek Ski Area toward Vail Ski Area. (Lou Dawson photo)

Continue on the packtrail as shown on the USGS *Red Cliff* map to the 9,680-foot level in the Two Elk Creek drainage. This is the base of Pete's Bowl to the south and China Bowl to the north. There is mediocre camping here in the trees to the south of the creek. Contact the Tenth Mountain Trails Association about a possible hut in this area (see Appendix C). To reverse the route, reverse the above directions. Vail ski area can be used for access.

Avalanche notes: Be careful of possible avalanches out of the Vail Bowls, especially while locating a campsite.

88 Pete's Bowl to Lime Creek

Difficulty: Intermediate
Time: 3 hours
Distance: 2 ½ miles
Elevation gain: 1,600 feet
Starting elevation: 9,680 feet
USGS 7.5 minute maps: Minturn, Red Cliff

Map—page 211

From the 9,680-foot level in the Two Elk Creek drainage, begin a climbing traverse up the hillside to the south that leads into the

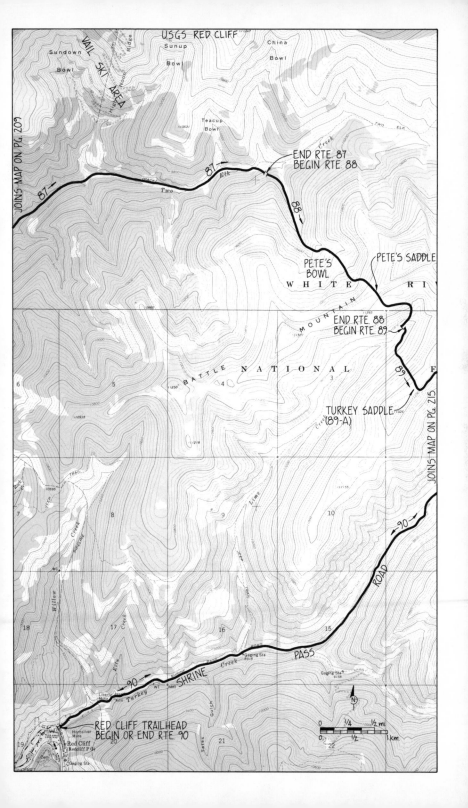

drainage of the bowl marked with the word "WHITE" on the USGS *Red Cliff* map. This is Pete's Bowl.

Follow the west side of the creek in Pete's Bowl to approximately the 10,300-foot level (stay out of the actual creek bed because the creek follows a steep-sided gulch). Cross the creek at approximately the 10,300-foot level and head up through open areas and glades in Pete's Bowl to the saddle between map Points 11,608 and 11,365 on the USGS *Red Cliff* map; this is called Pete's Saddle.

From Pete's Saddle drop down to the south to a good campsite at the 10,760 elevation in the Lime Creek drainage. Contact the Tenth Mountain Trail Association about a proposed hut here (see Appendix C).

To reverse the route, use the above directions. For alternative access, use the Vail Ski Area, or Lime Creek.

Avalanche notes: Be careful of the steep open slopes at the junction of Pete's Bowl and Two Elk Creek. Stay away from the steep avalanche slope forming the eastern exposure in Pete's Bowl. If the back bowls of the Vail Ski Area are closed, there may be some avalanche danger; check on this with the Vail Ski Area (see Appendix C).

89 Lime Creek to Vail Pass

Difficulty: Intermediate
Time: 7 hours
Distance: 6 ½ miles
Elevation gain: 1,000 feet from Lime Creek; 1,100 feet from Vail Pass
Starting elevation: 10,760 feet
USGS 7.5 minute maps: Red Cliff, Vail Pass

Map—page 215

From the 10,760-foot level in Lime Creek follow the Lime Creek logging road a short way up the ridge separating Lime Creek from Turkey Creek. Leave the logging road at the saddle (89-A) at 11,240 feet on the ridge, Turkey Saddle. From here intersect the Lime Creek logging road again as it contours at the 11,200-foot level, then gradually drops into the Turkey Creek drainage, and intersects the Shrine Pass Road (see Route 90). Ski the Shrine Pass Road over nondescript Shrine Pass and on to Vail Pass (see Route 90 and "Vail Pass Trailhead").

Top: *Signs indicating Shrine Pass.* Bottom: *Looking to the west at Shrine Pass. (Lou Dawson photos)*

An avalanche where people had recently skied. Extreme care is essential in avalanche terrain. (Lou Dawson photo)

For the return, begin at the Vail Pass Trailhead and reverse the above directions by skiing the snow-covered Shrine Pass Road up several switchbacks, then up a mile-long climb to a high point at 11,156 feet. From here continue to Shrine Pass. Take care to leave the Shrine Pass Road for the Lime Creek logging road at the 10,680-foot level (89-B) (see map in text). There is an obvious sign at this junction, but it might be covered by snow.

Avalanche notes: There are steep banks and open slopes on the Lime Creek logging road. These are fairly stable, but could be trouble during periods of extreme instability.

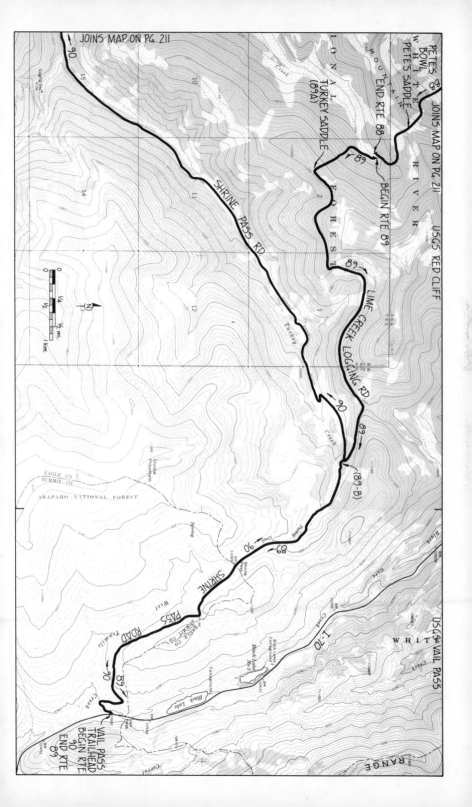

90   Vail Pass to Red Cliff via Shrine Pass Road

Difficulty: Intermediate
Time: 8 hours
Distance: 12 miles
Elevation gain: 580 feet
Starting elevation: 10,580 feet
USGS 7.5 minute maps: Red Cliff, Vail Pass

Maps—pages 211 and 215

The Tenth Mountain Trail from Lime Creek to Vail Pass (see Route 89) uses only a small section of the Shrine Pass Road. But the road is an excellent tour in its own right, and is good access to or from the town of Red Cliff (see "Red Cliff Trailhead"). Red Cliff is a good place to start or to end a Tenth Mountain Trail trip because there is lodging here (see Appendix C). The Shrine Pass Road is usually skied from Vail Pass (see "Vail Pass Trailhead") because of the minimal elevation gain and because of the nice cruise down to Red Cliff, but it is also a good trip from Red Cliff to Vail Pass. Either way, arrange a ride or leave a car at your ending point.

From Vail Pass, ski the snow-covered Shrine Pass Road up several switchbacks, then up a mile-long climb to the high point of the tour at 11,156 feet. From here ski a fairly flat mile to the actual Shrine Pass—really just a nondescript area of clearings. From Shrine Pass, ski the long gradual descent down Turkey Creek to Red Cliff.

To reverse the route, simply follow the signs in Red Cliff to the Shrine Pass Road. Ski the snow-covered road all the way to Vail Pass.

Avalanche notes: This is a fairly safe route. There is the possibility of small avalanches on some of the steeper open slopes. Take normal precautions.

LOUIS W. DAWSON II works as a homebuilder in the Aspen area when he's not out searching for ever new and challenging routes to ski the mountains of Colorado. Though born in New Jersey, Dawson answered the call of the hills early on and has lived in the Aspen area for 19 years. He's also an experienced mountain climber and a member of the American Alpine Club. Dawson has combined his climbing and ski-mountaineering expertise as an instructor for both Outward Bound and the National Outdoor Leadership School, and often works as a free-lance guide.

APPENDICES

Appendix A

Route Numbers Grouped According to Difficulty

Novice: 1, 14, 17, 18, 29, 34, 36, 37, 41, 42, 43, 46, 50, 59, 60, 61, 66, 73, 74

Intermediate: 2, 4, 5, 11, 16, 19, 28, 29, 33, 35, 38, 44, 45, 48, 51, 52, 55, 64, 65, 67, 72, 74, 78, 79, 80, 81, 82, 83, 84, 85, 86, 87, 88, 89, 90

Advanced: 3, 6, 7, 8, 9, 12, 13, 15, 16, 19, 20, 23, 24, 25, 26, 27, 29, 30, 31, 32, 39, 40, 44, 47, 49, 53, 54, 55, 56, 57, 58, 62, 63, 68, 69, 70, 71, 75, 76, 77

Extreme: 10, 21, 22, 55

The above difficulty ratings apply to the entirety of the routes described. In addition, the indicated segments of the following routes are suitable for very inexperienced skiers:

Route Number	Recommended Distance To Travel
1	Several miles
4	Several miles
7	To Cow Camp
11	To the Cabin
12	One mile
14	Stay on maintained trails
18	Two miles
32	Three miles
36	One mile from Red Mountain Roadhead
41	Up onto the CF&I shelf
43	Two miles
46	Two miles
50	Stay on maintained trails
51	One mile
57	Several miles
59	Stay in the campground
60	Several miles
61	Several miles
66	Stay near the highway
83	Several miles
92	Ski near Vail Pass or Red Cliff

Appendix B

Recommended Overnight Tours

ONE NIGHT OUT

Route Number	Difficulty	Route Number	Difficulty
4	intermediate	44	intermediate
4 + 5	intermediate	52	intermediate
6	advanced	52 + 53	advanced
7	advanced	56	advanced
7, 8 + 12	advanced	57	advanced
11	intermediate	61	novice
12	advanced	70	advanced
15	advanced	71	advanced
24	advanced	72	intermediate
29	novice near Sun Deck Restaurant	73	novice
		74	novice
		75	advanced
37	novice	76	advanced
39	advanced	77	advanced

TWO OR MORE NIGHTS OUT

Route Number	Difficulty
6	advanced
13	advanced
15 + 16	advanced
23	advanced
26	advanced
29 + 31	advanced
69	advanced

Appendix C

Trip Information: Names, Addresses and Phone Numbers

Emergency	Telephone Numbers
Eagle County Sheriff	(303)328-6611
Gunnison County Sheriff	(303)641-1113
Pitkin County Sheriff	(303)925-3232 or 911

Information

Forest Service: Aspen	(303)925-3445
Forest Service: Gunnison	(303)641-0471
Forest Service: Vail (Frisco office)	(303)668-5404
Vail Ski Area (Vail Associates)	(303)476-5601
Colorado Highway Patrol	(303)945-6198

Appendix C (Continued)

Forest Service: Vail (Frisco office) (303)668-5404
Vail Ski Area (Vail Associates) (303)476-5601
Colorado Highway Patrol (303)945-6198

Ski Council

Aspen Nordic Council (303)925-4790
P.O. Box 10815
Aspen, CO 81612

Guide Services

Aspen: Rocky Mountain Climbing School (303)925-7625
Crested Butte: Crested Butte Mountain
  Resort (303)349-2333
Vail: Crooked Creek Ski Touring
    Box 3142
    Vail, CO 81658

Maps

National Cartographic Information Center
United States Geological Survey
507 National Center
Reston, VA 22092

Huts

Fred Braun (303)925-7162
Hut Committee Chairman
302 West Main Street
Aspen, CO 81612

Friends Hut Inc.
Box 3055
Aspen, CO 81611

Tenth Mountain Trail Accommodations

Tenth Mountain Trail Association
  (hut reservations) (303)925-5775
1280 Ute Avenue
Aspen, CO 81612

Diamond J Ranch (Routes 80, 81, 82) (303)927-3222
26604 Frying Pan Road
Meredith, CO 81642

Crooked Creek Ski Touring (Routes 81, 82, 83, 84)
Box 3142
Vail, CO 81658

Turkey Creek Lodge (Routes 89, 90) (303)827-5513
Box 28
Red Cliff, CO 81649

Bibliography

AVALANCHE INFORMATION

Kelner, Alexis and Hanscom, David. *Wasatch Tours.* Salt Lake City: Wasatch Publishers, Inc., 1976.

LaChapelle, Edward R. *The ABC of Avalanche Safety,* 2nd ed. Seattle: The Mountaineers, 1985.

Perla, Ronald and Martinelli, M. *Avalanche Handbook.* Washington, D.C.: U.S. Department of Agriculture #489, 1976.

Williams, Knox and Armstrong, Betsy. *The Snowy Torrents—Avalanche Accidents in the United States 1972-1979.* Jackson, Wyoming: Teton Bookshop Publishing Company.

GENERAL SKI MOUNTAINEERING

Barnett, Steve. *Cross Country Downhill,* 3rd ed. Seattle: Pacific Search Press, 1983.

Bein, Vic. *Mountain Skiing.* Seattle: The Mountaineers, 1982.

Peters, Ed. *Mountaineering, the Freedom of the Hills,* 4th ed. Seattle: The Mountaineers, 1982.

Tejada-Flores, Lito. *Backcountry Skiing.* San Francisco: Sierra Club Books, 1981.

Watters, Ron. *Ski Camping.* San Francisco: Solstice Press/Chronicle Books, 1979.

GEOLOGY

Chronic, John. *Prairie, Peak and Plateau.* Denver: Colorado Geological Survey, 1972.

Young, Robert G., and Young, Joann W. *Colorado West.* USA: Wheelwright Press, Ltd., 1977.

ROUTE INFORMATION

Borneman, Walter, and Lampert, Lyndon. *A Climbing Guide to Colorado's Fourteeners.* Boulder: Pruett Publishing Company, 1978.

Eberhart, Perry, and Schmuck, Philip. *The Fourteeners.* Chicago: Swallow Press, 1970.

Wyrick, Ken. *Hiking Guide to Aspen.* Aspen: Aspen Editors, Inc., 1978.

SAFETY

Darvill, Fred T. *Mountaineering Medicine.* Mount Vernon, Washington: Mountain Rescue Unit, 1969.

Lathrop, Theodore. *Hypothermia: Killer of the Unprepared.* Portland: Mazamas, 1972.

Wilkerson, J. P. *Medicine for Mountaineering,* 3rd ed. Seattle: The Mountaineers, 1985.

INDEX